"Considering that only 18 percent of U.S. adults hold a passport in the face of rapid globalization, it only follows that to be truly educated, Americans must commit themselves to travel. Christian George resurrects the sadly neglected Christian practice of the pilgrimage, saying in effect that not only do we travel to know the world better, we need to take spiritual journeys in order to learn more about ourselves. *Sacred Travels* is a book that will convince you to hurry to renew your passport or rush to apply for one."

KAREN MAINS, director, *Journeys for Hungry Souls*

"If you are weary of 'religious fast food' and of competing on the 'fast track,' then slow down and walk awhile with Christian George. You will discover the richness of the authentic pilgrim life. This is a stimulating guidebook for pilgrims who are serious about making progress in the things that matter most."

WARREN W. WIERSBE, author and former general director, Back to the Bible

"For more than half a century I have been a pilgrim; yet only through Christian's insightful pen have the journeys suddenly come full course, especially in the spiritual realm. Interestingly I first met Christian George in the midst of one of his pilgrimages. Traveler or not, young or old, this brief but life-changing volume puts the world and its journeys into perspective! Interweaving travel experience, historical vignettes and personal observation, Christian has given his readers the map to an edifying pilgrimage."

DOROTHY KELLEY PATTERSON, professor of theology in women's studies, Southwestern Baptist Theological Seminary, Fort Worth, Texas

"Christian George has a pilgrim heart and a soul sensitive to the sacred. These reflections on his pilgrim journeys to sites of spiritual significance provide just the right combination of memoir and invitation to stir the pilgrim spirit in us all. This book is written with a gentle spirit that whispers, 'You come, too.'"

J. NORFLETTE DAY, associate professor of divinity in spiritual formation and New Testament, Beeson Divinity School

A man comes across an ancient enemy, beaten and left for dead. He lifts the wounded man onto the back of a donkey and takes him to an inn to tend to the man's recovery. Jesus tells this story and instructs those who are listening to "go and do likewise."

Likewise books explore a compassionate, active faith lived out in real time. When we're skeptical about the status quo, Likewise books challenge us to create culture responsibly. When we're confused about who we are and what we're supposed to be doing, Likewise books help us listen for God's voice. When we're discouraged by the troubled world we've inherited, Likewise books encourage us to hold onto hope.

In this life we will face challenges that demand our response. Likewise books face those challenges with us so we can act on faith.

LIKEWISE. *Go and do.*

SACRED
TRAVELS

Recovering the Ancient Practice of Pilgrimage

CHRISTIAN GEORGE

FOREWORD BY CALVIN MILLER

IVP Books

An imprint of InterVarsity Press
Downers Grove, Illinois

InterVarsity Press
P.O. Box 1400, Downers Grove, IL 60515-1426
World Wide Web: www.ivpress.com
E-mail: email@ivpress.com

InterVarsity Press® is the book-publishing division of InterVarsity Christian Fellowship/USA®, a student movement
active on campus at hundreds of universities, colleges and schools of nursing in the United States of America,
and a member movement of the International Fellowship of Evangelical Students. For information about local and
regional activities, write Public Relations Dept., InterVarsity Christian Fellowship/USA, 6400 Schroeder Rd.,
P.O. Box 7895, Madison, WI 53707-7895, or visit the IVCF website at <www.intervarsity.org>.

All Scripture quotations, unless otherwise indicated, are taken from the Holy Bible, New International Version®.
NIV®. Copyright ©1973, 1978, 1984 by International Bible Society. Used by permission of Zondervan Publishing
House. All rights reserved.

Design: Cindy Kiple

Images: road: Macduff Everton/Getty Images
globe: Nick Belton/istockphoto.com

ISBN-10: 0-8308-3502-4
ISBN-13: 978-0-8308-3502-7

Printed in the United States of America ∞

Library of Congress Cataloging-in-Publication Data

George, Christian Timothy, 1981-
  Sacred travels: recovering the ancient practice of pilgrimage/
  Christian Timothy George.
      p. cm
  Includes bibliographical references.
  ISBN-13: 978-0-8308-3502-7 (pbk.: alk. paper)
  ISBN-10: 0-8308-3502-4 (pbk.: alk. paper)
  1. Chistian pilgrims and pilgrimages—History. I. Title.
  BV5067.G46 2007
  263'.041—dc22

                                                                        2006030488

P   19   18   17   16   15   14   13   12   11   10   9   8   7   6   5   4   3   2   1
Y   22   21   20   19   18   17   16   15   14   13   12   11   10   09   08   07   06

For my father,
a pilgrim after God's own heart.

CONTENTS

O Thou,

God of all long desirous roaming,

Our hearts are sick of fruitless homing,

And crying after lost desire.

Hearten us onward! as with fire

Consuming dreams of other bliss.

The best Thou givest, giving this

Sufficient thing—to travel still

Over the plain, beyond the hill,

Unhesitating through the shade.

Amid the silence unafraid.

Till, at some sudden turn, one sees

Against the black and muttering trees

Thine altar, wonderfully white,

Among the Forests of the Night.

"THE SONG OF THE PILGRIMS"
RUPERT BROOKE

FOREWORD

Sacred Travels is a warm confessional written by a sojourner who has discovered the heart of God. It is in every sense a "moving" book. It has hidden within its pages a most glorious truth that all believers must recognize or never know the wonder of real togetherness with God. The truth is simple; the Almighty is not static. He moves through time, nations, lands and people. So often we visualize him on his great invincible, unmovable throne where he has been seated for solitary centuries, lovingly doting on his continents of grandchildren. Oh, sure, he may rise on an elbow from time to time to yawn or nap or hurl thunderbolts at miscreants. But much of the time he is a stay-at-home Jehovah.

Christian George reminds us in his own lyrical way that two-thirds of the word *God* is *go*. Those who see him as locked in heaven miss him altogether. The God at the center of Christian George's faith is on the move. He is stepping out through fields of martyrs, fiery convictions and postmodern individualism. He is still present in those places where he once walked, lingering in the winds that blow across the plains where the faithful once charted his presence in pillars of fire and clouds of smoke. As the Celts believed, he inhabits the "thin" places, where earth and heaven pass so close that his reality is tangible in the moment.

This ever-moving God is the center of this book. Christian George has made his own God Trek and found his heart strangely warmed. Now he wants us to make the journey with him. He is eager to show us the footprints where God once walked among his frightened followers and suited them up in the armor of advance.

The places you are about to visit were not notable before God walked there. They became notable because he walked there. Only after his visits did they become the sites of monuments and cathedrals. There, where the blood flowed, the flame danced in the darkness and martyrs sang their last hymns, God passed in the shadows. Those who saw him wept. But then time moved on. The cities came, the centuries ran down like wax, and we forgot that God had ever passed that way.

Thank God that Christian George poked around in the cold ashes and found the living embers of old sacrifices. In this book he has kindled yesterday's coals into new fire. He has relit the torch and these ancient altars hold once again the fire that we supposed was dead. As you turn the next few pages, strap on your seven-league boots. The walk is long but doable. In the process of walking you will become what both God and Christian would have you be: a pilgrim.

Calvin Miller
Beeson Divinity School
Birmingham, Alabama

INTRODUCTION

To Be a Pilgrim

He who would valiant be 'gainst all disaster,
Let him in constancy follow the Master.
There's no discouragement
shall make him once relent,
his first avowed intent
to be a pilgrim.

JOHN BUNYAN

"We can't name him that," my mother pleaded. "The poor child won't have a single friend in all the world!"

My father relented. "'Calvin Augustinus George' doesn't really roll off the tongue."

After pondering hundreds of baby names, they finally arrived at a decision. "We will name him for a pilgrim—Christian—from John Bunyan's book *Pilgrim's Progress*."

Pilgrim's Progress smells of prison, for it was written in one. Thrown in jail for preaching the gospel without a license, Bunyan wrote a story in his cell. It is a story about life's deepest questions, primarily, "What must I do to be saved?"

The story begins with a burden. Christian wakes up with a heavy load on his back. He doesn't know where it came from or what it means, and no matter how hard he tries, he cannot remove it. It is singed to his shoulders. To make matters worse, he reads in a book that his city is going to be destroyed with fire, and his family thinks he's crazy. But one day while he is walking through a field, a man named Evangelist points him in the right direction. He tells Christian of a city, a Celestial city, he must travel to. Unable to tolerate his burden any longer, Christian embarks on a journey.

Along the way he meets many characters—Worldly Wise Man, Goodwill, Hopeful, Faithful, Great-Heart. He travels through many terrains—a slough of despond, a hill of difficulty, a valley of the shadow of death. Sometimes he stays on the path, other times he strays. Demons plague him, friends betray him. But suddenly he sees a cross. It's on a hill far away but not out of reach. As Christian kneels before it, the burden on his back rolls away. He is overjoyed! At last, he's free! With a map in his hand and a skip in his step, Christian journeys home.

Pilgrim's Progress paints a picture of pilgrimage. Every element of the journey is smeared on the canvas: temptation, faith, forgiveness, danger, trust, courage, risk, friends, enemies, battles and victories. It represents a Christian's passage from death to life, from hate to love, from sin to grace. It teaches us about the burden of backsliding, the frustration of failing and the consequences of deviating from the straight and narrow path. In 1678, *Pilgrim's Progress* escaped the Bedford prison and began its own pilgrimage, traveling through the centuries as a bestselling Christian narrative.

In a society that struggles to discipline itself, Richard Foster's book *Celebration of Discipline* opens our eyes to the importance of spiritual exercise and inward conditioning. Why are spiritual practices so important? According to Foster, "The classical Disciplines of the spiritual life call us to move beyond surface living into the depths. They invite us to explore the inner caverns of the spiritual realm."[1] In a culture in which superficiality governs our lives and actions, spiritual disciplines urge us to reconsider what it means to be a Christian and a pilgrim.

Spiritual disciplines call us away from a bloated faith that doesn't let us squeeze the Savior into our schedules. They call us away from an anorexic faith in which we fail to absorb sufficient nutrients for spiritual health. They call us away from a bulimic faith that compels us to binge on Christian beliefs on Sunday morning but to purge them up on Monday morning. A regular diet of spiritual disciplines gives us the health we need for communion with God, the stamina we need to advance his kingdom, and the strength we need to battle the world, the flesh and the devil.

The purpose of this book is to introduce the body of Christ to the spiritual discipline of pilgrimage. Pilgrimage is an ancient practice in need of modern discovery—a physical, emotional and spiritual journey that goes inward, upward and outward.

We live in an age that sees people drowning in questions, searching for answers and starved for purpose. Pilgrimage is a spiritual practice that reminds us of our sacred purpose—to grow closer to God. Whether we choose to believe it, we are all on a journey. The trail winds and wiggles through this world, often obscured from view, but life's deepest questions are answered along its gravel.

Our culture craves immediate gratification—instant coffee, instant oatmeal, instant emails, instant messaging. Words like *patience*, *steadfastness* and *commitment* sound strange to us. We replace slow modems with high-speed Internet access. We refuse to drive the speed limit. We hate waiting two hours in the hot sun, even to ride a roller coaster. Fast food is not fast enough. Sermons are not short enough. The push of a button cooks our dinner and the twist of a knob dries our clothes.

Throughout the Gospels, Jesus frequently puts his schedule on pause to restore and rejuvenate his spirit. His disciples, too, are called to this task. Look at them. They are weary from preaching, teaching and healing all day. Their daily planners are bursting at the seams. But Jesus says, "Come with me by yourselves to a quiet place and get some rest" (Mark 6:31).

Two thousand years later, in a world burdened with busy schedules, Jesus invites us to take a journey. He asks us to depend on his guidance and navigation. He urges us to abandon our self-confidence and give ourselves to sacred serendipity. To this end, we sing with the hymnist B. B. McKinney, "Wherever he leads, I'll go."

According to Webster's Dictionary, a pilgrim is one who "journeys in foreign lands." As pilgrims we are not tourists, casually meandering through a city. Nor are we nomads, aimlessly wandering through the wilderness. We are sojourners, seekers of the city "whose architect and builder is God" (Hebrews 11:10). We might own a house, but it is more a hotel than a home. We might claim a nationality, but our true citizenship lies in heaven. We might drive to work every day, but our real journey is to Jesus. With Paul we press on to win the prize, homeward bound as if we belong to no other place. We live in a time of transition, pushed by the past, pulled by the future, but plastered to the present. Truly, we are strangers in this land.

Pilgrimage has long been a discipline for practitioners of the world's major religions. Muslims make pilgrimages to Mecca, Buddhists to Mount Kailash, Hindus to Kedarnath, Jews to Israel, and Christians to Rome. Pilgrimages occur even among those who are not affiliated with a religion. Some civic and secular destinations include the national monuments in Washington, D.C., the Eiffel Tower in Paris, the Colosseum in Rome, Stonehenge in England and the pyramids in Egypt. Pilgrimage is deeply rooted in the soil of the human soul. Life itself is a pilgrimage, and although most people recognize that they are on a journey, many travel without consciousness of their destination. These are pilgrims unaware, forced into the future by the ticking of the clock and dragged along by the winding chains of time.

Pilgrimage belongs to the deepest impulse of the evangelical tradition—reformation. A medieval theology incorrectly viewed pilgrimage as credits to a purgatory account—the more trips you take, the less time you bake. However, the grace-based theology rediscovered by Martin Luther and the other Reformers revises our understanding of pilgrimage as a discipline of sanctification, not justification. Pilgrimage does not save us. Rather, it is a grace that reminds us that salvation is a journey with Christ as our guide and heaven our goal.

Pilgrimage itself is undergoing its own reformation. Protestants are discovering it for the first time, and Catholics are recovering a biblical interpretation of it. Pilgrimage is ecumenical, uniting the entire body of Christ. There are many limbs in this body, each uniquely useful and beneficial, but they are all moving in the same direction. Heaven awaits the heel just as much as the head, hand and heart. Pilgrimage belongs to the whole Christian community, for its origins are found directly in Scripture. From Abraham to the exodus to the visit of the Magi, sacred journeys are deeply ingrained within the biblical narrative.

Pilgrimage is my passion. From a very early age I traveled the world with my father. Sometimes my mother and sister joined us for the journey, but most of the time, it was a father and son event. On our trips we visited missionaries and encouraged churches, and in our quest for spiritual discovery we found that God moves in many mysterious ways. He is active in other continents, and I quickly realized that the church is much bigger than I ever thought it could be.

We voyaged to distant lands and different cultures, to pilgrimage sites in dozens of countries. From mossy castles to ancient monasteries, we followed the footprints of thousands of pilgrims who had gone before. These adventures exposed me to other traditions within the spectrum of Christianity—limbs beneath the head of Christ I had never known. Their disciplines and customs were strange, but each one taught me something special about the Christian journey. They did not breach the walls of my denominational convictions; rather, they solidified them. Pilgrimage after pilgrimage, God grew bigger in my eyes, more transcendent, multicultural and internationally involved. One day I realized that the children's song was right: he really does have the whole world in his hands.

In this book are my most meaningful pilgrimages—memories that have defined and refined me, sacred travels that have opened my eyes to a global Christianity and a global God. I invite you to walk with me through Europe, Asia and Great Britain; through Protestant, Catholic and Celtic traditions. Along the way, may we discover again what it means to be a pilgrim.

PILGRIMS IN THE PROCESS

Preparing to Journey

The journey of a thousand miles begins with one step.

LAO TZU (570-490 B.C.)

Canterbury Cathedral, England, 1170

Death arrived for him on a cold December day. The scene was set, the swords unsheathed, and Thomas à Becket knelt before the angry knights. Through snow and sleet they had come, four of them, to rid the world of this meddlesome priest. Their wish would soon become reality.

Born in London, Becket was the son of a successful English merchant. He was privileged in all the ways of wealth—sent to Paris to be educated and back to England to join the household of Theobold, archbishop of Canterbury. His intelligence, charm and wit won Becket much favor, and after studying law, he was promoted to archdeacon of Canterbury. The newly crowned King Henry II befriended Becket. He named him his chancellor, ordained him to the priesthood and, after Theobold's death, gave him the honor of becoming archbishop of Canterbury.

All was well until Henry broke friendship with Becket over political differences. Becket soon became an enemy of the empire and fled to France for six years of exile. Eventually, he and Henry met in Normandy and appeared to reconcile, upon which Becket returned to England. But then Henry, still in France, found out that Becket had excommunicated the bishops of London and Salisbury for their support of the king, and he was filled with rage. "Who will rid me of this meddlesome priest?" he asked. Four zealous knights sailed across the English Channel, stormed into Canterbury Cathedral and found Becket kneeling in prayer upon the altar.

"I am prepared to die for my Lord," he whispered. He bent his neck toward the blade. After receiving countless strikes from the sword, Becket lay dead on the altar. "We can leave this place," one of the knights exclaimed. "He will not get up again."

After the martyrdom of Thomas à Becket, things began to happen at Canterbury Cathedral. Healings, miracles and strange phenomena were reported near Becket's tomb in the crypt. As the cathedral's reputation spread across England, a small shrine was constructed behind the altar where he was slain, and this site has drawn hordes of pilgrims during the past eight hundred years. In the Middle Ages, Canterbury Cathedral became the most popular pilgrimage site in England, rivaling even the great sites in Italy, Spain, France and Israel. Hundreds of thousands of peasants left their farms and pastures to travel across country and continent to Canterbury in hopes of finding healing, forgiveness and blessing.

Canterbury Cathedral, England, 1995

With bags in hand and passports in pockets, we entered the Birmingham, Alabama, airport. I was fourteen, had curly brown hair, and was trying to put some muscle on my body. Having been bitten by the lost luggage bug before, my father and I packed lightly—a few clothes, a great pair of shoes and, of course, some extra rolls of toilet paper (never trust a British bathroom).

"Next in line," said the security guard.

It was my turn, and I walked through the metal detector.

Beep, beep, beep!

"Sir, I'm going to have to ask you to step over here and spread your legs."

"Excuse me? Spread my legs?"

"That's right, sir. It's standard procedure."

I didn't want to. I was a pilgrim, not a terrorist. But for security's sake, I acquiesced to the awkward pat-down. Perhaps it was a small price to pay for being a pilgrim in the age of modernity. After being manhandled, I picked up my suitcase from the x-ray belt and headed on my way.

"Sir, I'm going to have to ask you to open that for me," the security guard said.

I groaned.

In front of everyone, the security guard unzipped my suitcase and exposed six mega-sized rolls of baby-soft, extra-scented, fluffy white toilet paper. "God, have mercy on my soul," I prayed, watching a smile break out on his face. It was a smile that said, "Hey, man, what's with all the toilet paper?" I cringed. He accidentally knocked a roll onto the floor and I bent down to pick it up, panicked that someone had seen my secret stash. Good grief. What a way to start a pilgrimage!

To Canterbury Cathedral we were bound. The hum of the airplane engines and the long flight over the Atlantic provided me a pleasant opportunity to read about its history and tradition. In A.D. 43, the city of Canterbury was nothing more than a small Roman outpost called *Durovernum Cantiacorum*, built after Emperor Claudius invaded England. The original foundations of a Roman wall and theater can still be seen in the city. Saint Augustine, a Benedictine monk sent by Pope Gregory I to convert the Anglo-Saxons, visited Canterbury in A.D. 597 and established a monastery there. After becoming the first archbishop of England, Saint Augustine built a cathedral in Canterbury that has stood the test of time, remaining the primary ecclesiastical administrative center of England, the mother church of the Diocese of Canterbury, and a place of international interest for its renowned pilgrimage heritage.

I reached into my suitcase and pulled out Geoffrey Chaucer's *Canterbury Tales*. Inspired by the enormous popularity of pilgrimage to Canterbury in his time, Chaucer told a story about a group of pilgrims traveling to see the shrine of Thomas à Becket. Its Prologue reads:

When April with his showers sweet with fruit
the drought of March has pierced unto the root . . .
Then do folk long to go on pilgrimage,
and palmers to go seeking out strange strands,
o distant shrines well known in sundry lands.
And specially from every shire's end
of England they to Canterbury wend,
the holy blessed martyr there to seek
who helped them when they lay so ill and weak.[1]

Between pockets of turbulence and in-flight movies, I read the poetic pages. Every pilgrim in the book had a story: the Knight, the Miller, the Cook, the Monk, the Priest, the Wife of Bath. Some were polite, others uncouth. Some I found fascinating, others a bit bland. But one thing they all shared—pilgrimage. They had embarked with different reasons and motivations, and yet they were unified in their common direction. One by one they swapped stories, recounted memories and exchanged adventures of days gone by. The book became more than a book to me; it became something alive and transformative.

It's one thing to read a book about other people's pilgrimages to Canterbury, but it is quite another to actually be on a pilgrimage to Canterbury. I guess it's the difference between looking at the moon as an astronomer and going to the moon as an astronaut. As I read the *Canterbury Tales* and grew to love its characters, something strange swept over me. I realized that the pilgrimage I was taking to Canterbury stood in direct continuity with all pilgrimages ever taken to Canterbury. I was following an ancient set of footprints to a place of mystery and great history.

Our airplane kissed the runway and I breathed a sigh of relief. I was severely jet-lagged and cramped from the ride, and the excitement of reaching Canterbury Cathedral had been building within me for eight long hours. I thought of past pilgrims who traveled for months by foot, buggy and boat before beholding the sacred site. For them, a pilgrimage to Canterbury would have been the trip of a lifetime, its anticipation overwhelming, its cost sacrificial.

From London we traveled by train to Canterbury. Through green pastures we sped, flying past small houses and beautiful landscapes. After a quick lunch, we walked to the cathedral, wide-eyed, humbled and speechless. The large, double western towers jutted into the sky, piercing it as if to protect its pilgrims from the hostility of wind and weather. The main church formed the nucleus of the complex, the cloister and monastic quarters to the north side. On the east and west sides were buildings reserved for purposes of hospitality, catering to the needs of paupers, peasants and pilgrims.

We entered the cathedral, feeling a sudden sense of antiquity. The perpendicular nave and its soaring arches pulled our eyes upward, raising our gaze almost to God himself.

On slabs of stone we walked, joining the millions of feet that had previously smoothed them. Time itself was forgotten, an irrelevant element of nature discarded at the entrance of the church. The burning candles, the smell of incense, the melodic harmonies of the chant. All these belonged to an ancient tradition of worship that brought us into a state of sacred simplicity and reminded us that we walk lowly on this earth.

The shrine that marked the spot of the martyrdom of Saint Thomas was destroyed during the Reformation under the orders of King Henry VIII, but a simple description in brass and a candle remain. In Trinity Chapel we discovered two detailed accounts of Becket's life, represented by twelve stained glass windows. These windows brought to mind how the knights who murdered him said that he would never get up again, but in a way, he has risen indeed. What rose above his place of execution far exceeded his earthly influence, and it lingers to this day as a place of peace and holy consecration.

I enjoyed studying the individual panes of stained glass about the martyr's life. The colors were riveting, almost mesmerizing. During the Middle Ages, when literacy was at an all-time low, stained glass windows became the "poor man's Bible." Illustrated accounts of biblical narratives were communicated not with ink but with art—the gospel ingrained in glass. As light poured through the windows of the cathedral, the stories of Christ and the truths of the Scriptures permeated the hearts of thousands of uneducated peasants. For them, if God was to be grasped, he would be found shining through the stories of the windows.

I've heard it said that being a Christian is reflecting God to the world, much like the moon reflects the sun. But as I stared at these windows, a thought struck me. Perhaps Christians refract the light of God more than just reflect it. As we encounter Christ and the transforming power of his presence, it does not merely ricochet off us as light bounces off the moon. It passes right through us. Through the spectrum of individuality and uniqueness, we refract the light of God. We are windows to the world, colorful and varied yet, like the characters of Chaucer's tales, grainy and flawed.

In his letter to the Ephesians, Paul describes how the wisdom of God is communicated to the world. He uses the word *polypoikilos*: "His intent was that now, through the church, the manifold wisdom of God (*hē polypoikilos sofia tou theou*) should be made known to the rulers and authorities in the heavenly realms" (Ephesians 3:10). This is the same root word used in the Septuagint to describe Joseph's coat of many colors: "Now Israel loved Joseph more than any of his other sons . . . and he made a richly ornamented robe (*chitōna poikilon*) for him" (Genesis 37:3). This word means many-sided, multifaceted, varied, colorful.

Too often I am tempted to smear the coat of my Christianity through the blood of an animal like Joseph's brothers did, insisting that it be uniform. But what can an artist paint with just one pigment? When seen under the microscope, the church is splintered by race, segregated by culture and divided by denomination. But when viewed from afar, the individual panes of color transform into a great work of art, the mosaic becomes the masterpiece, and the warmth of God travels to the world through multicolored windows.

We still had much to see in Canterbury—the crypt, the cloister and the paintings—but I retired to a wooden chair in hopes of soaking up the last bit of beauty in the sanctuary. The chair squeaked under me, bearing the load of another weary pilgrim. As people passed by I watched their expressions. Modern eyes callously used to skyscrapers and superdomes opened in childlike wonder upon seeing this ancient sanctuary. Perhaps these travelers were shocked by the ornate architecture or stunned by the striking novelty. But perhaps they had come, as I had, as pilgrims, hoping that the silent stones would somehow teach them something sacred about themselves, about their past and about the God who holds the future.

PRACTICING PILGRIMAGE

Pilgrimage is practiced in many ways. For some, a morning walk with a warm cup of coffee is enough. Others enjoy longer retreats to places of spiritual nourishment, refreshment and isolation. An expensive trip to Europe or Asia is certainly not required; pilgrimage is a discipline for anyone and everyone, wherever you live and whatever you do. Richard Foster writes, "God intends the Disciplines of the spiritual life to be for ordinary human beings: people who have jobs, who care for children, who wash dishes and mow lawns."[2] Pilgrimage is not limited by location.

Nor is pilgrimage about when, where or how we go. It's about why we go. Pilgrimage expands the horizons of our faith and gives us a greater understanding of our own spiritual journey. While ancient in origin, pilgrimage is relevant today for many reasons. It moves us from certainty to dependence, it helps us discover God's involvement in human history, it challenges and stimulates our faith, and it invigorates us to be like our Lord in thought, word, deed and devotion. Pilgrimage is an outward demonstration of an inward calling—to follow Christ, wherever the steps may lead. For hearts that hunger to escape the chaos and find the quiet, pilgrimage is a proven discipline.

Many Christians practice pilgrimage, but due to its typically Muslim and Eastern religious associations, some shy away from calling themselves pilgrims. Peter reminds us, however, that as Christians we are "aliens and strangers in the world" (1 Peter 2:11). Here, the Greek word for "strangers" is *parepidemous*, which transformed from *peregrini* to *pelegrim* in Latin, and eventually to *pilgrim* in English. Pilgrimage affirms our calling to live as aliens and strangers in this land, and when it is properly practiced, each adventure deepens our understanding of the God who calls us to be in this world but not of it.

All Christians, no matter their stage in life, can benefit from the discipline of pilgrimage. For children learning their ABCs, it fixes Christianity in their minds by painting a visual picture of the Christian journey to heaven. For college students backpacking across a continent, it transforms an ordinary summer adventure into an extraordinary spiritual revival. For married couples adjusting to the joys of living together, it unites them in purpose and partnership. What about those who cannot travel—those who are elderly or hospitalized, or those who are physically disabled? Can they practice pilgrimage?

Yes. Some of my greatest pilgrimages have been in the hospital moments of my life. Lying on my back with an IV in one hand and a Bible in the other, I traveled through the Old Testament. I visited Joseph in his jail, Daniel in his den and Solomon in his sanctuary. I plunged beneath the Mediterranean Sea and heard Jonah wailing for a way out of that fish. I touched the slimy seaweed, tasted the bitter saltwater and brushed against the eely creatures of the deep. And when I came up for air, I was tired. The New Testament would have to wait until tomorrow.

Pilgrimage is centered around one thing—progression. God does not call us to be static saints, even if we cannot move physically. We are constantly on the move spiritually, evolving in our understanding of God, chasing him in our prayers, crawling and climbing over obstacles and challenges. No specific location is holier than another, though different places may provide particular opportunities to encounter God in fresh ways. We agree with Oswald Chambers that "the reality of God's presence is not dependent on any place, but only dependent upon the determination to set the Lord always before us."[3] Because the presence of God extends everywhere, even unto the very ends of the earth, pilgrimage can be practiced by anyone, anywhere, anytime.

First steps are always the hardest. Just look at a baby. Her first steps involve shaky legs and lots of falling down. But gradually, step by awkward step, her muscles strengthen and her confidence builds, and then walking becomes as natural as breathing. The discipline of pilgrimage is like this. We begin on our knees, inwardly confessing our spiritual condition before God. We like sheep have strayed from the Shepherd, crawling away from our Creator as fast as we can. But the Shepherd gets on his hands and knees and crawls after us, not satisfied until we are safe. Eventually, we want spiritual steak instead of spiritual milk, and crawling no longer gets us where we want to go. We learn the arts of jogging, hopping and running, and pilgrimage becomes a holistic discipline, motivating our heels as well as our heads and hearts. It shapes us into three-dimensional Christians—Christians who inwardly recognize our sin, upwardly commune with Christ and outwardly follow in his footsteps. Pilgrimage is a discipline for the soul and the sole.

Prodigal Pilgrims

I have a confession: my gardening skills stink. Sure, I can go to Wal-Mart, buy a plant, dig a hole and throw some water on it. That's not hard. But real gardening requires skill, patience and diligence. A real gardener spends hours on hands and knees, planting seeds, inspecting leaves and pulling weeds.

My mother is a real gardener. With hands caked with soil, she faithfully waters roses, plants orchids and cuts chrysanthemums. (The only things I liked cutting in the garden were worms. They really do stay alive!) In the middle of our garden, my mother grew a plant called the "touch-me-not." Now, if you are as gardenally challenged as I am, you might be unfamiliar with this plant. According to the Encyclopædia Britannica, the petals of the touch-me-not, or *impatiens balsamina,* burst under the slightest pressure. When squeezed, their seeds explode and fall to the ground. The Latin name is related to the word "impatient" because of the plant's eagerness to purge its seeds.

My mother would remind me, often with her eyes more than her lips, "Christian, stay away from the touch-me-nots. You can touch any plant in the whole garden. You can pick the peppers and eat the strawberries, but stay away from the touch-me-nots."

Yeah, right. On a Tuesday evening around five o'clock (the moment is marked well in my memory) my mother had gone to run errands, and there I was, staring through the window at the touch-me-nots. What a perplexing plant—a forbidden fruit. As I walked through the garden I heard the wind, or perhaps a chirping bird, or quite possibly a slithering serpent, say these words: "Go ahead, Adam, eat that apple!"

And I did. The moment my fingers touched the touch-me-nots their bulbs exploded and their seeds fell to the ground. One by one, I purged the contents of the petals, laughing at the little bulbs. But I didn't laugh for long. When my momma came home that evening, I realized that I had disobeyed the gardener, and soon I would pay the price. And after a little discussion and a lot of reflection, I considered making a sign that said "Spank-Me-Not" to place on the back of my britches!

Pilgrimage began in the garden of Eden. It was the Shepherd's original design to lay us down in green pastures. But when Adam and Eve touched the touch-me-nots, humanity was driven from the garden to the desert. Nature's perfect balance was tilted, and the cosmos was contaminated. Before their very eyes, the universe withered.

Like every great drama, however, the plot did not end after Act I. God in his grace still had the main character, Jesus Christ, to introduce to the audience. Through his atoning work on the cross, a path was paved back to paradise. A highway to heaven was restored. And suddenly, pilgrimage was possible.

Though Christians visit places like Canterbury Cathedral, we are all aimed at another destination—a divine destination—a garden greater than anything we've got in this galaxy. But we are not there yet. The gravel has yet to turn to gold beneath our feet. We are traveling in transition, imperfect, unbalanced, unfinished creatures who long for renewal and yearn for completeness. We are pilgrims in the process.

O Almighty God, who hast called us to faith in thee, and hast compassed us about with so great a cloud of witnesses; grant that we, encouraged by the good examples of thy Saints . . . may persevere in running the race that is set before us.

BOOK OF COMMON PRAYER (1928)

THE DESERT OCEAN

Swimming Against the Stream

Hear my cry, O God. . . . Lead me to the Rock that is higher than I.

DAVID, PSALM 61:1-2

Somewhere over the Atlantic Ocean, May 1927

The cockpit was cramped, but the dream was enormous—to fly from New York to Paris nonstop. It had never before been done. Charles Lindbergh had been flying for twenty-eight hours in his plane, and with low spirits he checked his watch.

If his calculations were correct, the green coast of Ireland should be minutes away. He tilted the plane, the Spirit of St. Louis, to the left, glancing down at the smooth, blue ocean. The waves were peaceful, rising and sinking like the belly of a sleeping giant. But if his calculations were incorrect, and if Europe was further east than he expected, the sleeping sea would rouse and swallow him inside his flying coffin.

The weary aviator urged his engine onward, hoping it would pull him faster to the shore. It still amazed him how two shaky wings and a fickle engine could keep five thousand pounds of metal in the air. He watched the fuel gauge and anxiously lowered his altitude to one hundred feet above the surface of the water. He was low enough to see the masts of fishing boats, but high enough to avoid hitting them.

Suddenly, a mountain appeared before him, but its shape and size surprised him. Jutting seven hundred feet out of the water, Skellig (Irish for "rock") Michael lay in his path. He pulled on his instruments and avoided a collision, breathing a sigh of relief that land was not far away. The long journey across the rough Atlantic was over, and after nearly thirty hours of traveling, Charles Lindbergh had become the first person in history to complete a nonstop transatlantic flight.

Port Magee, Ireland, August 2004

It was a dangerous journey—too dangerous, in fact, for me to recommend. While Charles Lindbergh approached Skellig Michael by plane, we came to it by boat. The pilgrimage is so marked in my memory that sometimes at night I can still feel the wild movement of that boat, tossing us up and down like an empty can in the hands of an angry ocean.

As a boy, I often fished in the Tennessee River with my grandfather. The water never scared me, even though I knew what swam in it (we once caught a sixty-pound beast of a catfish). But we were not in Tennessee, and the North Atlantic Ocean was certainly not a river. Two thousand miles away, on the same line of latitude as Skellig Michael, the Titanic, the ship "that God himself could not sink," had made her home on the ocean floor.

By the lines carved in his face, I knew that Captain Owen knew the sea. For more than two decades he had been taking pilgrims from Port Magee to Skellig Michael in his dual-engine, thirty-foot orange boat. His father, too, was a captain, and a good one. He had taught Owen everything he knew about the North Atlantic—the fifty-foot waves, the unexpected currents and, of course, the misconception that a clear, sunny sky meant great sailing weather.

Five hundred years after the birth of Christ, Christians came to Skellig Michael and built a monastery on its summit. At that time it was popular to mimic Saint Anthony, a pilgrim who retreated to the African desert to preserve a Christianity that was being contaminated by secularized Roman society. In the desert, Anthony gave himself to a life of discipline, meditation and solitude. His influence spread across the plains of Europe to England, Wales and eventually Ireland. Irish monks of the sixth century did not have a desert to flee to, but they did have an ocean. Skellig Michael was the most distant island of the known world, the last bit of earth one could stand on before falling off the flat edge.

Twelve of us were making this journey in the boat. After climbing down an iron ladder (from which I almost fell), I stepped onto the deck. Captain Owen was preparing to set sail, and he was dressed for the water. Thick, brown rubber boots hugged his heels, and a bright yellow jacket protected his body. I wanted a word with him before we left.

"So the water will be calm today?" I asked, looking at the cloudless sky.

His thick Irish accent disarmed me. "No, lad. The stomach of the ocean is upset today. I hope you don't mind getting wet."

I waited for the punch line. Kept waiting.

"We'll be lucky if all twelve of us can make it to the island!" he said.

"But the water is so calm," I replied. "Look, there's not even a ripple out here!"

Captain Owen looked. Then smiled. I started praying. "Oh, great God Almighty; let this man be joking!"

"Young lad," he said, "I hope you had a small breakfast."

He was serious, and I was scared. Returning to my seat I thought of home, family and friends. I thought of all the castles I wanted to see, the books I wanted to read, the goals I wanted to accomplish. Would I live to see them? I looked down at the water, its ripples mocking me, daring me to continue on the pilgrimage.

My father and I had brought a friend with us on this trip. His name was David Riker, and he had studied all over the world, including Beeson Divinity School in Alabama, Kings College in London, and the University of Aberdeen in Scotland. His passion for history, theology and pilgrimage had aided us on many a journey, and his presence was a blessing in many difficult circumstances.

David sat next to me near the back of the boat. He, too, was experienced with rivers, as he was originally from Brazil. "On the Amazon," he once told me, "there are dangerous, cow-eating fish. They travel in packs, and if they see you, Christian, they will eat you. We call them *piranha*, the 'toothed fish.'" As we pushed out to sea, I could only imagine what giant, eely, man-eating creatures were swimming beneath our boat.

I looked back at the shore. The green hills of Ireland were greener than I'd ever seen. Every imaginable shade was visible from the water—forest green, lima bean green, Granny Smith apple green. I saw shades of green I never knew existed. It was like God had cut the grass of the earth and spread its shavings across the hills of Ireland.

But we were leaving those hills behind, venturing into the blue unknown. The sun was scorching my neck and the gasoline fumes were burning my throat, but the gentle rocking of the boat calmed my nerves and settled my stomach. *What's all the hype about, anyway?* I wondered. *I don't see any waves.*

Up—down—splash! Up—down—splash! Up—down—splash! Now there were waves. I turned on my video camera in hopes of capturing footage for a Discovery Channel special: "When Nature Goes Terribly Wrong," "When Sea Creatures Emerge" or the like. Soon the passengers, including myself, were being tossed from our seats as the waves hurled our boat in every direction. All my unconfessed sins rushed to the tip of my lips—every mistake, every lie, every thought. *Up—down—splash! Up—down—splash! Up—down—splash!*

I thought of Jonah. Perhaps my former transgressions were causing this turbulent water. Perhaps I had rebelled against God and this was the fateful result. If I were thrown overboard, the sea might subside and the other pilgrims on board could still be saved. I looked at the blackish, foamy deep. Enormous, scaly creatures were surely waiting beneath the waves, eager to eat me for breakfast. The sea had never looked so hungry, and I decided it was best to remain in the boat.

My heart experienced a boxing match between fear and faith for one sea-sickening hour. At the top of a wave, when I could see the horizon, faith emerged victorious and there was hope. But when the boat slammed into the depths and I bounced off the edge of my seat, fear regained control. We closed our eyes. "God, when will it end?"

Jesus, too, was once in a boat. The water was white with foam and his disciples were white with fear. The waves mounted, the thunder clapped, and the boat was breaking to pieces. Yet Jesus, the creator of the clouds and sustainer of the seasons, was asleep beneath the bow. This thought soothed me as I tossed around on top of the Atlantic. Even asleep, God was in control. And if a sleepy Savior could awake from a dream to hush the nightmares of his disciples, surely he could calm my fears too. What was water, anyway, but two humble hydrogens and one obedient oxygen?

"There she is!" yelled the captain, aiming his finger at Skellig Michael. The sight was startling. No, it was more than that—it was paralyzing. Skellig Michael is the top of an underwater mountain, rising like a phoenix from its ocean ashes. White, squawking birds circled our boat. From their nests on the side of Skellig Michael they dove into the water, perhaps chasing some fleeting fish. We docked against the port, disembarked and said a hearty prayer of thanksgiving for our safe arrival. At last. Something solid to stand on. Something that could not sway or sink.

In A.D. 825, Viking Norsemen from Scandinavia also docked at Skellig Michael. They hiked up the rocky coast, kidnapped the abbot of the monastery and eventually starved him to death. Stealing, murder and torture were games the Vikings loved to play, and monasteries were primary targets since they housed elaborately decorated manuscripts embellished with jewels, precious metals and rare pigments. During a raid, it was customary for the Vikings to strip off their clothes, douse themselves with grease and murder anyone in their path. The monks who lived on Skellig Michael kept death very near their eyes, judging every action, word and deed by it. They understood the brevity of life and the eternal nature of the world to come.

During the Dark Ages, Skellig Michael was a lighthouse to the world. Literacy was low among the people of Europe, but the monks who lived on the island faithfully translated the Scriptures and preserved the Christian tradition. They worked in rooms called *scriptoria*, engraving the Gospels not only in words but also with art. Colorful Celtic animals and meticulous details were painted onto the pages, reflecting the monks' respect for the written Word of God as well as the unique way the Bible had influenced the Celtic tradition. It is true that the Irish "saved civilization" by preserving the ancient texts, and they also reintroduced them to Europe through faithful missionary endeavors.

As I hiked up the base of Skellig Michael, I marveled at the unique rock formations surrounding our path. The sea had no doubt done this, gnawing on the island with its ferocious North Atlantic waves. Captain Owen informed me that from time to time, tidal waves had risen so high that they swept right over the mountain, purging it of pilgrims as nature sometimes can.

As we arrived at the trail leading to the top of the island, I looked up at the vertical path. The view could have been taken directly from Jurassic Park or some other island that time had long forgotten. Legend has it that when Saint Patrick came to this island, with the help of Michael the Archangel he threw all the Irish demons into the heart of the sea. But I wouldn't have been surprised if one or two of them still resided on these rocks. What protection did we have from a deranged demon raptor who darted down the mountain looking for a pilgrim to snack on? I inched closer to the other pilgrims, hoping a dinosaur would eat one of them instead of me.

A thousand-year-old stairway took us to the top of the island where the monastery was located. Six hundred cracked and weathered steps held us to the hills—not an easy climb! At times, the path was only two or three feet wide and, when wet, it was extremely slippery. One little accident, a slight slip of the sole, and the poor pilgrim would get an up-close look at the sharp rocks hundreds of feet below. Several people in history could testify to this fall, were they alive to do so.

As we tried to keep our balance on the shaky steps, birds swarmed around us as they had done for thousands of years—playing and soaring without regard for time, appointments or deadlines—or gravity. I would have been less concerned about falling off the cliff were it not for the thirty-mile-an-hour wind gusts that slammed into us at all the wrong moments. "Oh, God," I prayed, "keep me on the straight and narrow path!"

David was the first to reach the summit, then my father. My camera-happy tendencies held me up, not to mention my fear of heights. At times, I actually crawled on hands and knees up the rigorous slope. Better safe than sorry.

A stone archway welcomed us into the safety of the small but sturdy remains of the monastic edifice. The three of us rested beneath its shade and rehearsed the Apostles' Creed, one of the oldest confessions in Christian history. Our legs were weary, our lungs were wheezy, and our cheeks were rosy red from the blistering gusts of wind. But we had arrived.

Six beehive huts, two chapels and an ancient, overgrown cemetery composed the monastic settlement. I was baffled by the huts, the rocky igloos that had sheltered the monks. How on earth could they have carried these stones up this mountain? How could they have survived the biting cold of winter, the constant threat of Vikings and the fact that civilization was horizons away? There was even a small plot of land where they harvested vegetables. Historians say the monks brought cows and sheep to Skellig Michael, but one by one they fell off its slopes—not entirely surprising.

I walked into a roofless, rocky chapel. So strange and old. There I was, three thousand miles from my home, standing on the top of a remote island surrounded by flying birds, jagged rocks and the sound of water crashing against the stones. Yet within the crumbling walls of this ancient church, I felt at home. I shared a common heritage with the hermits who worshiped in this room. My fears were their fears. My prayers were their prayers. My creeds were their creeds. My Christ was their Christ.

It rained cats and dogs (or maybe cows and sheep) as we marched down the side of Skellig Michael. By the grace of God I'm not still up there waiting for a chopper to take me to safety. The boat ride back to Port Magee was as volatile as the first, though Captain Owen cut us a fine pathway through the chop. When our boat had ventured several miles out, I looked back at the island dissolving in the distance. Would I ever return to this sacred rock? Would I again behold its beauty? Perhaps. At least in my dreams.

Our boat docked against the port, and I thanked Captain Owen for the ride. Never had land looked so lovely! I scurried back to my hotel room, exhausted. My bed awaited with soft sheets and eiderdown. Depleted of energy and ready to snooze, I crashed onto its mattress. What a perilous pilgrimage we'd made, a spiritually challenging, emotionally draining, physically stretching adventure. We were only on the island for two hours, but I knew it would take a lifetime to unpack its spiritual blessings. I opened my Bible. A pilgrim named Paul lulled me to sleep with his letter to Rome: "For I am convinced . . . that neither height nor depth, nor anything else in all creation, will be able to separate us from the love of God that is in Christ Jesus our Lord" (Romans 8:38-39).

Perhaps it is safest to explore Skellig Michael with the imagination. Perhaps with Charles Lindbergh, it is better to admire it from the sky. But if you can survive the sea, and if you can climb the cliffs, a precious pearl awaits you, a treasure that hundreds of pilgrims have discovered, floating at the ends of the earth.

Every once in a while, when I close my eyes to pray, I go to that stony chapel secluded in the middle of nowhere. When life seems overwhelming, bills never ending and deadlines fast approaching, I'll secretly escape to that hidden place of mystery, that ancient island where austere monks took their burdens to the Lord and left them there. And I'll be home again.

Couch-Potato Christianity

Despite evidence to the contrary in the form of my pilgrimage to Skellig Michael, vegetating is one of my favorite activities. Give me a call, bring over a video, and it could be days before I see the sunshine.

I know I am not alone.

Have we become a culture of couch potatoes? As you might expect, the answer is yes. According to the Nielsen Company, the average American watches nearly four hours of television each day—that's fifty-two days of nonstop TV-watching per year. While the physical and spiritual muscles of our society are atrophying, our faith is not immune to this spiritual stagnation.

Pilgrimage is a revolutionary way of expressing our faith. It moves us out of our comfort zones and challenges us to think clearly about our calling. By taking us away from everyday luxuries, pilgrimage teaches us about the essentials. It teaches us that faith is risky and reminds us to be light on our feet. A pilgrim's pockets are never very full. We bring only what is needed for the journey and discard anything that hinders or weighs us down. We regain the early apostolic attitude toward possessions and become freer from the burdens of greed and selfishness.

Jesus came to comfort the afflicted. His ministry led him to the sewers of society where lepers and prostitutes received his comfort. But Jesus also came to afflict the comfortable. The rich young ruler, for example, had a comfortable stash of cash. Knowing the contents of both his heart and his wallet, Jesus told him to go sell his possessions, give the money to the poor, and then he could become a follower (Matthew 19:21). But the rich young ruler could not follow God because his comforts were his christ.

Salmon are interesting creatures. Compelled by instinct, they swim as sojourners against the stream, fighting currents and leaping waterfalls until they reach their spawning grounds. Other fish probably make fun of them. Perhaps the trout, bass and cod question the legitimacy of their journey. But the salmon does not care. "We refuse to go with the flow," they say. "Our gills are restless until they find their rest upstream."

Christians, too, are upstream animals. The journey is sloped, the destination is difficult, and the passage is unpopular. Made for motion, Christians aim their gills at God, traveling onward and upward. The fickle flow of society does not faze them. The changing currents of culture do not sway them. They are paddling pilgrims, following the path wherever it leads. Sometimes it leads to quiet waters, and other times it leads up raging rivers. But one thing is certain: the path will lead them home.

Jesus told Peter and Andrew they would become fishers of men (Mark 1:17). Can you imagine the expressions on their faces? Fishing for people? What a thought! But with nets of love outstretched, they caught a score of people for Christ. The discipline of pilgrimage opens our eyes to a world that is heading for a waterfall. The rapids are rough, and many are swept over the edge. But there is hope in the ripples, for Jesus says, "Come to me, all you who are weary and burdened, and I will give you rest" (Matthew 11:28).

Rest is most appreciated by those who work. In the same way, a week of pilgrimage gives meaning to the ordinary hours of our lives by reminding us that we were made for both exploration and rejuvenation. After returning from a sacred travel, I remind myself that resting is reserved for spiritual reflection. I often use this season of stillness to diagnose my spiritual condition. What has God taught me on this last trip? How have I been spiritually encouraged, equipped and challenged? With these questions brewing in the back of my brain, I can unwind and appreciate the mundane aspects of my life without worrying that I am drifting into laxity and spiritual rust.

Like Charles Lindbergh's flight across the Atlantic, pilgrimage invites us to take risks. While God might not move the mountain (or the ocean), he will certainly give us grace to climb it (or swim it). No matter how hard life hits, how deeply it cuts or how low it takes us, we can be confident that God has given us a map in the form of the Holy Scriptures, a guide in the Holy Spirit, and the promise that he will never leave us or forsake us. With these treasures hidden in our hearts, we can continue up the stream. Dangers may confront us and demons may attack us, but the God who has brought us this far will not forsake us now. Whether our pilgrimages lead through dangerous oceans or peaceful streams, the trip is worth the trouble and will mash up a couch-potato spirituality.

Christ with me, Christ before me, Christ behind me;
Christ within me, Christ beneath me, Christ above me;
Christ to right of me, Christ to left of me;
Christ in my lying, Christ in my sitting, Christ in my rising;
Christ in the heart of all who think of me,
Christ on the tongue of all who speak of me,
Christ in the eye of all who see me,
Christ in the ear of all who hear me.

SAINT PATRICK

IN THE STEPS OF LUTHER

Finding Refuge from the Storm

If I rest, I rust.

MARTIN LUTHER

Near Stotterheim, Germany, July 2, 1505
Claps of thunder split the clouds, and bolts of lightning burst the skies. A rainstorm brewed above the German landscape. It was a typical afternoon shower, the kind that cools the soil after the sun has baked it. But for young Martin Luther, the experience was explosive and terrifying.

"The storm will kill me!" he screamed, stumbling to the ground. Waves of rain scourged him in the soggy pasture. His life was full of storms, showers of conviction by day and tempests of depression by night. Swirling clouds of guilt and shame hung above his head, and no matter how fast he ran, no matter how far he went, he could never escape the fact that he was a raw and weary sinner, running away from a good and righteous God.

Luther questioned everything. Why am I on this earth? What will I do with my life? Is there a plan for me? After receiving a master of arts degree in Erfurt, Germany, he planned to follow his father's wishes and study law. He had the mechanics of a fine lawyer—a sharp mind, an honest heart and a strong command of grammar, rhetoric and Aristotelian logic. Yet Luther's heavenly Father had other plans for him—plans of transformation, education and reformation.

Perhaps God will send the storm away if I swear an oath to him, Luther thought. *I would rather be alive and oath-bound than dead and hell-bound!* Against the roar of the wind, Luther yelled, "I will become a monk!" It was an oath that would change his life forever.

Wartburg Castle, Eisenach, Germany, 1996

The steps of Luther led us along a windy path. He was a man on the move—running for his life, fleeing affliction, kidnapped by his friends. My father and I followed him from Eisleben where he was born, to Eisenach and Erfurt where he studied, to Wittenberg where he taught, and finally to the Wartburg Castle where he translated the Greek New Testament into the German vernacular.

Bats, bats, bats! Soaring, swooping and screeching. The annoying vampires of the night flew tirelessly outside our hotel window, untouched by the weight of gravity and unbound by the laws of civilization. Sleep was certainly out of the question, and I put a pillow over my head, praying for a little peace and quiet. "God, give me a break from the bats!"

Luther knew these bats. They tormented him, too, while he was here. Late at night as he wrote by the light of a candle, the little demons distracted him from the work of the Lord. My father and I had come to the Wartburg Castle of our own volition, but Luther had been kidnapped by his friend, Frederick III of Saxony, and brought to this place against his will for protection.

And did he ever need it! Nailing his ninety-five theses to the church door in Wittenberg had struck a nerve, shall we say, with the Catholic authorities. He was excommunicated by the pope and outlawed by the emperor, and many would have liked to see him burn for his beliefs. Luther insisted on *sola fides* (faith alone), *sola gratia* (grace alone) and *sola scriptura* (Scripture alone)—doctrines that invited harsh criticism from those who were endorsing indulgences and merit-based salvific teachings. For these reasons, he sat in seclusion from May 1521 until March 1522, far from the dangers of cruelty, torture and death.

Wartburg Castle is nestled in the heart of the Thuringian Forest. Its massive walls tower over the steeples of Eisenach, a small German town where the great musician Johann Sebastian Bach was born and the great novelist Fritz Reuter died. The castle hill was fortified as early as 1067. Over the next two hundred years, it was embellished and frequented by poets, musicians and artists. It became the seat of a lively court, a place of enjoyment with a festive atmosphere of entertainment and relaxation.

Climbing its hill, however, is anything but relaxing. Up and up we went, legs cramping, backs bending, lungs heaving. Never had I wished more ardently that lungs were filled with helium instead of oxygen! My faithful backpack, which I have taken on almost all my pilgrimages, bore heavily on my shoulders, and were it not for Luther's stay at this castle, I might have been tempted to chuck it all and take a taxi to the train station.

But Luther did stay here. He grew a beard, wore a cloak and dagger, went on hunts and even called himself Junker Jörg (Knight George). The walls of the castle protected him against the threats of the world and perhaps even inspired the words of his most famous hymn, "A Mighty Fortress Is Our God." For Luther, the lofty ledges of Wartburg reminded him that God is, as the psalmist writes, "my rock, my fortress and my deliverer" (Psalm 18:2).

No one needed delivering more than Luther. No one needed rescuing more than he. And like a caterpillar protected by a stone cocoon, Luther's words became his wings—words that enabled him to carry the translated gospel throughout the German geography.

Vivienne Hull once wrote, "Unlike mere travel, a pilgrimage is a journey into the landscape of the soul."[1] As the road to Wartburg Castle went upward, my thoughts went inward and I began to examine the landscape of my own soul. I questioned my Christianity. What if the path before me dissolved and I was left searching for God in the gravel? What if I woke up one morning and everything I'd placed my hope in had been proved false? Was I on track with God? Could I be confident in my salvation? Deep contemplation accompanied me up the 1,230 feet of that castle cliff, and when I arrived at the summit, I reached the conclusion that perhaps the beauty of faith lies in the blindness of life.

A medieval drawbridge connects the pilgrim to Wartburg Castle. It provides the only access to the castle and hasn't changed in appearance since the time of Luther. We crossed its planks, much like Luther did, except that he was blindfolded, probably bound and secretly smuggled in a buggy. Because of Luther's residency here, many pilgrims have climbed this mountain and carved their names into the sides of the castle; some of the inscriptions date back to the 1600s.

Inside the fortress is a small courtyard. The architecture of the surrounding buildings and houses reflects the Romanesque, Gothic and Renaissance eras. Many of them have been perfectly preserved and restored, including an ancient well. During the 1530s and 1540s, the dungeon of the south tower held a large number of Anabaptists, including Fritz Erbe, who carved his signature into the prison wall with the bone of his finger.

But we had not come primarily to the Wartburg Castle for Anabaptists or architecture. We came to set our eyes on Luther's study, the room where he spent many lonely days incognito, translating the Bible. I stood at the entrance of the musty room, still catching my breath from the long hike up the hill. Its layout is simple, no more than ten feet by twenty feet. On the left side of the room a small window provides a spectacular view of the German mountains. By day Luther must have loved this view, but at night the window was ravished by bats as they whispered sweet nothings of evil against the pane.

On the floor next to the window lies a bleached whale vertebra that Luther used as a sitting stool. It rises only about a foot from the floor and must have been about as comfortable as it sounds. Above it stands a medieval working desk that resembles the original one Luther used. On the other side of the room, a large green heater fills the space. Unfortunately, my eye had to travel farther than my foot, as red laser beams prevent the pilgrim from actually entering the room.

I stood at its entrance, gazing at the pictures of Luther hanging above the desk. Oh that these wooden walls could talk! I would ask them many things. I would want to know the faces they'd seen and the stories they'd heard, but primarily I would ask them about the epic battle between Luther and the devil that took place within their dark walls.

The year was 1522. Luther dipped his pen into the ink. Eleven weeks had passed since he began translating the Bible, and the project was almost complete. Although his work would enrage the papacy and infuriate the devil, at least the peasant would be able to read the Scriptures like the priest.

A shadow slithered across the room. It was a familiar shadow, a shadow that had tormented him since he was a child.

"I know I am a sinner!" Luther screamed. "Leave me alone!"

The demon snarled. "You are worse than that, Luther. Your mouth is filthy and your work is useless. God could never use a creature like you."

Luther knew his warts. He cursed like a sailor, drank like a fish, and if he ever owned his temper, it did not take him long to lose it.

Bats smashed against the window. "You will die in this castle," screamed the shadow.

Luther had heard enough. The trembling reformer grabbed a well of ink and hurled it at the devil. It soared across the room and exploded against the wall, splattering ink everywhere. Knight George had slayed his dragon, and the creature disappeared into the darkness.

Luther's original ink stain has long since vanished. Many fingers have faded the wall behind the heater, and some pilgrims have even taken pieces of it as relics. But every year someone, perhaps a castle custodian, secretly splashes the wall with a fresh coat of ink in hopes of keeping Luther's legacy alive.

I walked away from the entrance of the study not at all excited about the long descent down to the base of the hill, but eager to engage my own demons and, in so doing, to become a greater threat to the kingdom of Satan. Luther's hymn declares:

> And though this world with devils filled
> Should threaten to undo us,
> We will not fear, for God hath willed
> His truth to triumph through us.

The Prince of Darkness grim,
We tremble not for him,
His rage we can endure,
For lo, his doom is sure,
One little word shall fell him.[2]

My pilgrimage to Wartburg Castle taught me many things. It taught me the importance of packing lightly. It taught me that great friction usually precedes great movement. But above all, it taught me that being a Christian is like being a sirloin—sometimes God's got to marinate us. In general, I don't eat a lot of steak (seminary and poverty tend to go hand in hand), but I do know that my favorite steaks are marinated and filled with flavor before they're cooked.

Pilgrimage is a marinating process. The Bible is bursting with people who traveled to places of retreat where God seasoned and tenderized them, preparing them to take the next step of the journey. Moses marinated in the desert for forty years before leading the Israelites to the Promised Land. The apostle Paul marinated in the Arabian desert for three years before becoming the missionary of the millennium. Even Jesus spent forty days and nights marinating in the wilderness, dueling with the devil before beginning his public ministry.

There are seasons of life in which God pulls us into the stillness. Our lives are saturated with speed and we often get into the habit of working so hard, playing so much and praying so little that we become callous to our consciences. It is then that God takes us somewhere sacred and marinates us. God seasoned Luther in a castle, but others go on weekend retreats, extended job assignments or summer vacations. Some find marinating in outdoor explorations like hiking and camping, but wherever God takes us to marinate, whether it is across the sea or across the street, we can be confident that he has purpose for us there. Pilgrimage is a journey into the landscape of the soul, and when we return, we will be spiritually seasoned and refreshed for service in the kingdom of God.

JESUS, THE REFORMER

Pilgrimage is not only our journey to God, it is also God's journey to us. No matter how many steps we take to find him, he has already taken a thousand to us. And for a brief moment in history, Jesus Christ, the Creator, marinated with humanity.

I once heard a college English major talk about the incarnation. I don't remember his name, but I'll never forget his words: "In the beginning was the Word, and the Word was with God and the Word was God. And God took that precious Word, removed its heavenly italics, froze it in human font, and plunged it from its paragraph in paradise into the simple sentence of an earthly stable. And the Word became flesh."

Why did Christ take the ultimate plunge? What motivated his pilgrimage? Could it be that Jesus sought to reform us? The Jews had become so legalistic in dealing with the law of God that they missed the entire reason God had given it to them. From the beginning God worked to separate a people for himself, and Jesus reminded his audience that it was their motives that isolated them from other cultures, not just their actions.

Jesus came to reform the heart of his creatures because humans were always the apple of God's eye. Our spiritual journey did not begin at our conception, birth, conversion or baptism. It began long ago, before computers, automobiles and airplanes. Before nations were established and cities constructed. Before oceans were introduced to shores. Before stars swirled through galaxies. Even before the ticking of time itself, when nothing covered everything, there was God, thinking of us.

I met my wife, Rebecca, in our college cafeteria. The sky outside was blue. She was wearing pink. And in that moment of providential appointment, as I gazed over the glass of chocolate milk sitting on my tray, I discovered in her eyes the meaning behind all those sappy love songs: "Fly me to the moon and let me play among the stars. Let me see what spring is like on Jupiter and Mars." When I came back down to earth, I realized that my humpty-dumpty heart had fallen for her like the great walls of Jericho, and I never wanted the pieces to be glued together without her. It was a love that began at first sight.

But God's love is different. God loved us before we ever had eyes to see him, ears to hear him or lips to praise him. He took hold of us before we could even hold a pacifier. While we were crying in our cribs, Christ entertained us with his love. We agree with St. Anselm, "Lord my God, you have formed and reformed me."[3]

The beloved disciple John, while he was marinating on the island of Patmos, wrote that the Lamb was slain before the foundation of the world (Revelation 13:8). In other words, Christ was cemented to the cross before the world began turning on its axis. The blueprints for the crucifixion were already sketched in the mind of God, the dimensions of the cross already calculated, the length of the nails already measured, the seeds for the thorns already sown. And as the star of Bethlehem rose in the midnight sky, the King of Creation took a pilgrimage to our planet, just the way he planned it. From the celestial to the terrestrial, Jesus' journey was aimed at one wooden thing—the cross of Calvary. And with Martin Luther, we can sing:

> Did we in our own strength confide,
> Our striving would be losing;
> Were not the right Man on our side,
> The Man of God's own choosing.
> Doest ask who that may be?
> Christ Jesus it is He;
> Lord Sabaoth, His name,
> From age to age the same,
> And He must win the battle.

My Lord Jesus Christ, You are indeed the only Shepherd, and I, sorry to say, am the lost and straying sheep. I am anxious and afraid. Gladly would I be devout and cling to you, my gracious God, and so have peace in my heart. I learn that you are as anxious for me as I am for you. I am eager to know how I can come to you for help. Anxiously, you desire above all else to bring me back to yourself again. Then come to me. Seek and find me. Help me also to come to you and praise and honor you forever.

MARTIN LUTHER

THE WAY TO ASSISI

Toward Transparency

Thus says the Lord:
"Stand by the roads, and look, and ask for the ancient paths,
where the good way is; and walk in it, and find rest for your souls."

JEREMIAH 6:16 (ESV)

Assisi, Italy, 1206
Adrenaline rushed through his veins. Priests, lawyers and friends watched him, waiting to see what he would do. Would he repay the money he stole from his father—money he intended to give to the poor people of Assisi? Or would he refuse and weather his father's wrath? His destiny hinged on his decision.

Francis, originally named Giovanni Bernardone, was a medieval man. Fascinated by King Arthur and the Knights of the Round Table, much of his early life was spent pursuing romantic passions—dreaming about damsels in distress; fighting for honor, gold and glory; enjoying the luxuries of art and literature. This fascination, coupled with his desire for military success, drove him to the battlefield where he joined a military expedition against Perugia.

Clothed in chain mail, Francis gripped his sword, eager to engage the enemy and defend his town's honor. The hiss of flying arrows and the shouts of soldiers filled the air as Francis's army was overrun and hunted down like animals for slaughter. Fearing for his life, Francis could not believe his eyes. Dead and bleeding bodies were scattered across the plains. Daggers, axes and pikes were thrust in his face, and Francis was eventually forced to surrender. His dreams of chivalry and grandeur lay hacked to pieces on the ground, along with the limbs of his closest friends. The harsh reality of war replaced his youthful quest for knighthood, and at the end of the day he was dragged through the streets of Perugia as a prisoner of war.

His prison cell was damp and dark, and privacy was a luxury of long ago. Francis yearned for home; he was a spoiled kid, after all. Through fields of wheat he once walked, soaking up the blistering Italian sun. Fortunately for Francis, his father's pockets were deep, and after a year of grumbling cellmates, nostalgic nights and intolerable bouts with tuberculosis, a ransom was paid for his release. Being the son of a wealthy merchant certainly had its benefits.

Upon his return Francis lived licentiously. Decadent parties filled his days and nights. But God was slowly working in his heart, pulling him away from himself. Riches lost their luster and earthly vanities vanished. One by one, Francis traded his worldly habits for godly disciplines—party for prayer, dancing for devotion and celebration for contemplation. He even began to fast. And like the dawning of a sunrise, questions illuminated his cerebral sky. "How can I grow closer to God? Should I beg for food instead of buying it? What does creation teach me about the Creator?" Francis was unable to find the answers to his questions in Assisi, and in 1206 he embarked on a pilgrimage to Rome.

Although the height of the Roman Empire had long since passed, its spiritual intrigue remained. People wanted to see the bones of Peter, the underground catacombs and the sacred relics of ancient saints. Francis was no exception. As he crossed the Tiber River and entered Saint Peter's Basilica, he threw a handful of change into the grate near the altar. On his way out he encountered a begging man pleading for money. Moved to great compassion, Francis asked the beggar to exchange clothes with him. This took little convincing since Francis was dressed well. As the day progressed, Francis

subjected himself to the humiliation of begging in the streets, quite the opposite experience of his silver-spooned childhood. After returning home, his
heart grew sympathetic toward those who lacked material assets. He knew
that Jesus, too, was poor, without even a place to lay his head.

With the intention of providing for the poor, Francis sold his father's fab-
rics and textiles and gave the money away. According to Francis, this was
evangelism, but according to his father, it was robbery. Francis was caught
and condemned, and as he faced the court to settle the dispute, he knew that
discipline and estrangement waited if he did not cooperate with his father.
The tension intensified.

"I will gladly give back the money that belongs to my father," Francis
said, stepping forward with his purse. A sigh of relief swept through the audience, and a smile spread across his father's face.

"And not only do I surrender the money," he continued, "but take my
clothes too!" Francis stripped off his cloak, pants and shirt. Jaws dropped.
Naked for all to see, Francis placed his clothes on top of the moneybag.

His father was furious. Why would his son give away his future, not to
mention his clothes, to lead a life of poverty? He had raised him better than
that!

Francis looked into his father's eyes. "Up until this moment," he said, "I
have called Pietro di Bernadone my father. But now, I acknowledge only my
Father who is in heaven."

Picking up the purse and clothes, his father walked away, crushed and
disbelieving. The crowd, many of whom had benefited from Francis's gen-
erosity, was moved to tears, and they wrapped him in their clothes. Francis
had proven his point. For him, poverty was more important than possessions, dependency more desirable than autonomy. He continued to pursue
an aggressive spiritual transformation and dove deeply into the mysteries
of God.

Francis's spiritual fervor intensified and his godly reputation spread
widely. No matter where he went or what he did, his words, actions and ambitions were welcomed. The poverty of his Christianity became so attractive

that many people mimicked his lifestyle. Eventually, Franciscan monasticism was born.

Near the end of his life, Francis found himself in Egypt traveling during the time of a crusade. In his youth, such an opportunity would have been the pinnacle of his Arthurian dreams for military notoriety. But his devotion to God and his yearning for peace had changed the contours of his heart, and instead of bringing a sword of death, Francis offered a message of life. A Muslim sultan noticed Francis and was so impressed by his peaceful demeanor that he allowed him safe passage back to his home in Italy.

While some aspects of Francis's life are difficult to believe—stigmata, wolf taming and preaching to birds—it must be acknowledged that those who take Jesus' Beatitudes as seriously as Francis did are not bound by the regulations of normality. Saint Francis lived almost a thousand years ago, but his legacy of love and faithful devotion to God lingers to this day.

Assisi, Italy, 1999

Across painted plains we went. With Florence behind and Assisi before us, we rushed along the tracks, continuing our great adventure. I unzipped my backpack and pulled out a book on Saint Francis of Assisi, along with a half-eaten turkey and Swiss sandwich. They went well together, the sandwich and the saint, but by the time we reached our destination I was ready for a quiet evening, a big bed and a very hot shower.

The shower was cold and the bed was small, but the view from our balcony window was breathtaking—endless green and yellow fields crushed beneath the blue Italian sky. It was a view to make van Gogh's mouth water. Situated in the Perugia province on the western flank of Mount Subasio, the cobblestone streets of Assisi rise from the flat, wheat-laced landscape almost symbolically, like a monk with hands stretched to heaven. Saint Francis must have loved it here.

The city of Assisi supports itself with small manufacturing industries such as embroidery, but its main income is from tourists and pilgrims who go out of their way to see where Saint Francis was born and lived. The city

boasts an Umbrian, Etruscan and Roman heritage. The Romans called it As-
sisium and built a temple within its walls dedicated to Minerva, the Roman
goddess of handicrafts, arts and, eventually, war. While some believe that
Assisi was first introduced to the gospel only two decades after the death and
resurrection of Jesus, it is more probable that Christianity came here in the
third century through the preaching and heroism of Saint Rufino, a coura-
geous Christian who was drowned for his faith in the Chiascio River. By A.D.
412, as Christianity spread throughout the Roman Empire, the memory of
Rufino was recovered and the gospel that he faithfully preached took root in
the city.

The most notable landmark in Assisi is the church and convent of Saint
Francesco, constructed after the death and canonization of Francis. Beautiful frescoes fill the walls of the upper and lower churches of the basilica,
along with scenes from Francis's life painted by Giotto, one of the most important Italian artists of the fourteenth century. Having just come from Florence we were certainly in the mood to see good art, but due to recent dam-
age from an earthquake in 1997, the basilica was closed the day we
arrived—along with the tomb of Saint Francis in a small chapel in its crypt.

The following morning, our friend David, my father and I set out to explore. Even with a good map we got lost, roaming from one zigzaggy street
to another. We visited the Cathedral of Saint Rufino, the church that once
was a temple to Minerva, and the Sanctuary of Saint Damiano, and we ate
gelato in the main square. But eventually we found our destination. It was a
tiny museum—a wooden door—unassuming and not well advertised.
Owned and operated by Franciscan nuns, the museum welcomes pilgrims
of all faiths. Wooden crosses, relics and postcards can be purchased at the
counter, but as we soon discovered, there is a deeper treasure hidden beneath this museum.

One of the Franciscan sisters approached us and struck up a conversation. We told her about our interest in Assisi and how we had traveled from
Alabama to see his home. She told us about her work in the museum, her
life as a nun and the reasons for her conversion. Then, after a cordial and

informative chat, she asked us to follow her into the next room. We followed. Down steep, concrete stairs we went, sinking into the cold basement beneath the museum.

At the base of the staircase, a rocky wall greeted us, smelling of earth and history. It was here, she told us, that in 1182 Saint Francis was born. We stared at the rock, still a bit unsettled from the abrupt change of venue. Could this really be the spot where he was born? After giving us a brief history of the museum and how it was built on this rock, the nun agreed to say the Lord's Prayer with us. It seemed appropriate at the time to pray this ancient prayer in such a sacred place. We joined hands, bowed heads and closed eyes. Two Americans, a Brazilian and an Italian nun. And God showed up.

It always amazes me how great things often come from humble beginnings. Who would have thought that a man like Francis, a great hero and leader in the Christian faith, would have been born in the small, rural city of Assisi? Or Martin Luther, the translator of the Scriptures and reformer of the church, born in the small town of Eisleben? Or Saint Teresa, founder of the Discalced Carmelites and the first saint ever to be made a doctor of the church, born in Avila, Spain? Big things do come in small packages, and the question lingers today, "Can anything good come out of Nazareth?" After we concluded the Lord's Prayer beneath the floor of that museum, I looked over at my father, who himself came from the ashes of Chattanooga, and I felt honored to be his son.

My father is the most amazing man I've ever known. Born in 1950 in one of the worst parts of Chattanooga, Tennessee, he lived in abject poverty with a disabled mother and an abusive father who died in prison when my dad was twelve. He was called to preach at age eleven and served his first church, Fellowship Baptist Church in Chickamauga, while a college student. Eventually he pursued his master of divinity and doctor of theology degrees at Harvard and taught at the Southern Baptist Theological Seminary in Louisville, Kentucky, where I was born. He is now the founding dean of Beeson Divinity School in Birmingham, Alabama.

Most kids grow up thinking their dads are invincible, infallible and, for the most part, immortal. But when the teenage years come around, they see their father's faults and realize that he's not immune to mistakes. Though everyone falls short of God's glory, I still retain a sense of wonder when it comes to my dad. I am as tall as he is now, but I look up to him as one of the greatest individuals God is using in the church today, and no matter how old I get, I will always see my dad through the eyes of a little child who thinks his daddy is the biggest man in all the world.

Another great hero of the faith, Henri Nouwen, a spiritual thinker and writer, once said, "Ministry is, first of all, receiving God's blessing from those to whom we minister. It is a glimpse of the face of God."[1] These words were carved by years of experience when Nouwen left his teaching post at a university to work with handicapped people in the French community of L'Arche. Under the conviction that "we cannot live a spiritual life alone,"[2] he sought work with men and women who could not thank or repay him for his kindness and compassion. Like Francis, Nouwen's heart went out to the poor, and by becoming poor himself, he was able to write, "The more you have loved and have allowed yourself to suffer because of your love, the more you will be able to let your heart grow wider and deeper."[3]

Henri Nouwen and Francis of Assisi speak with great power to our secular and religiously privatized culture. They challenge us to divorce ourselves from the magnetism of materialism and the selfishness of individualism. Following in the footprints of Christ, they remind us that the kingdom of heaven belongs not to the self-sufficient or the independent but rather to the poor in spirit, those whose real needs can be met only by a selfless Savior.

Our pilgrimage to Assisi exposed my deep attachments to things that ultimately have no value. It revealed my love of possessions—my unwillingness to hold them loosely—as I compared my luxurious life to the austerity of Saint Francis. But it also exposed my theological shortcomings. While reflecting on the life, teaching and example of Saint Francis, I was confronted with a simple but somewhat unresolved question: What does it really mean to know God?

Some claim that it is impossible to really know God, at least personally. Others claim that we can believe in God but cannot justify loving him because he is either powerless over the evil in the world or cruel for allowing it to exist. There are still others, like myself, who believe in God and worship him, but all too often do so casually and without great conviction. In fact, according to a recent Barna survey on worship, most people say after attending a church service that "they did not experience the presence of God during the service."[4]

Francis confronts our casual Christianity by challenging us to engage God completely with all our heart, strength, mind and soul. By example, he shows us that true freedom is found in vulnerability, real worship, transparency and genuine joy—a lifestyle that is given to simplicity, dependency and community.

We left Assisi only one day after arriving. It was a short stay, but certainly not a forgettable one. Our pilgrimage across Europe had to continue, and like the children in C. S. Lewis's *The Lion, the Witch and the Wardrobe,* we stepped onto the train as through a magical closet. And we were back in the reality we once had known.

TOWARD TRANSPARENCY

The discipline of pilgrimage is a journey into the depths of the heart. Occasionally when I take a spiritual retreat or pilgrimage, I come across a prayer garden. Within this garden is often a small stone labyrinth. Its purpose is simple yet profound: to lead the pilgrim to the center. As I walk the narrow trail, back and forth between the windy rocks, each step I take leads me closer to the center of the circle. This prayer garden is a tool used to train the mind to focus on God and eliminate the distractions of the world. Pilgrimage, too, is a tool that helps us get at the center of who we are, why we are here and where we are going.

But pilgrimage is also an upward discipline, ushering us into the presence of God. It is a means of grace, a vertical adventure into sacred communion with the Savior. Pilgrimage strips off the garments that keep us from spiritual familiarity with God. Layer by layer it unclothes us. First, our shoes of self-reliance are removed, followed by our gloves of greed and materialism. Then our vests of vanity fall off, followed by our belts of boasting. And when on the journey only our underwear of independence remains, we know that transparency is not far away. When that, too, is finally discarded, we stand with Saint Francis before our Heavenly Father completely vulnerable, totally exposed and ready to be clothed with robes of righteousness.

For about ten grueling months of my life, I worked in the fast food industry. I had several jobs at this particular restaurant: deveining frozen chicken breasts, cleaning smelly toilets and deep fryers, and taking out the trash. (I washed my hands between each task—don't worry.)

Of the three jobs, my favorite was taking out trash. Sometimes the trash bags would explode, but most of the time it was a great way to get outside for some fresh air. Every time I left the building, however, something strange would happen: it didn't matter how fast I walked or how much trash I had in my hands, to the people I passed in the drive-through line, I was invisible. They looked right through me. To them I was a transparent trash boy.

Being transparent before God, though, is not about invisibility; it's about vulnerability. It's about getting rid of everything that blocks our communion with God—sin, doubt, guilt, shame, pride, lust, all of it. Pilgrimage helps us practice being vulnerable before God, but it also helps us purge the trash in our lives. It shows us the festering places of our faith and helps us amputate our spiritual shortcomings. Since traveling requires tremendous sacrifice, faithful discipline and extreme flexibility, pilgrimage exposes us to ourselves. It also opens our eyes to a world of invisible people—people who are overlooked and underprivileged. In their eyes we see ourselves most clearly.

Perhaps life is like a solar system. Some people experience God up close and intimately. With Saint Francis they live on Mercury, burning in and breathing up the fiery fellowship of God. Others travel farther from the sun like comets, feeling the warmth of God maybe once or twice in a lifetime. Still others are so removed from the true source of light that they are frozen in their knowledge of the holy. These are Pluto pilgrims, icy and isolated.

Others prefer living on earth—not too hot, not too cold. But no matter where we are in the solar system of sanctification, Francis would teach us that God seeks to have us closer. He is pulling us into the proximity of his love. Day after day, step after step, we are invited to live in sacred intimacy with the Eternal.

Lord, make me an instrument of your peace.
Where there is hatred, let me sow love;
where there is injury, pardon;
where there is doubt, faith;
where there is darkness, light;
where there is sadness, joy.

O Divine Master, grant that I may not so much
    seek to be consoled as to console;
to be understood as to understand;
to be loved as to love;
for it is in giving that we receive;
it is in pardoning that we are pardoned;
it is in dying that we are born to eternal life.

FRANCIS OF ASSISI

IN SEARCH OF SPURGEON

A Pilgrim's Perspective

By perseverance the snail reached the ark.

CHARLES SPURGEON

Colchester, England, 1849

The streets of Colchester were frozen beneath a thick blanket of snow. Charles Haddon Spurgeon looked out the window; he hated cold weather. In fact, later in his life he often retreated to a tropical resort in France to escape the bitter, biting London winters. He enjoyed the warmth of gardens, palm trees and crystal blue waters. But at fifteen, Charles was stuck in Colchester. And it was cold.

His grandfather, the Reverend James Spurgeon, was a preacher and fine storyteller whose tales had intrigued young Charles during his childhood. They were stories about castles, dragons and bravery. They were stories about knights in shining armor and damsels in distress. Charles would never forget his grandfather's stories, especially the scary ones.

"There is a pit," his grandfather once said, "a dark, bottomless hole in the earth where people fall forever."

Charles perked with interest. "They fall forever?" he asked.

"Forever and ever!"

Charles's eyes grew wide.

"If you listen close enough you can almost hear them screaming." Reverend Spurgeon put his hand to his ear. "Do you hear them, Charles?"

Charles shook his head.

"One falling soul looks to another and asks, 'Are you near the bottom yet?' 'No,' the other soul replies, 'I've been falling for a hundred million years, and I will always fall, for this is the bottomless pit!'"

Charles chuckled. "Why are these people falling?"

"They are falling away because they did not know God."

Charles hated heights. "I don't want to fall into that pit!" he declared.

"And so you won't, dear boy, and so you won't." His grandfather smiled and placed Charles on his knee. "God has great plans for you, young lad. One day, he will use you to bring a great revival in this land."

Charles thought about that story as he watched the blizzard through the window. As a young child he had discovered a copy of *Pilgrim's Progress* in his grandfather's attic, and it soon became his favorite book. He felt like Christian, bogged with burdens. *What must I do to be saved?* he wondered. *Perhaps I will find my answer in church.* Putting on his coat and boots, he prepared himself for a Sunday morning journey.

Ice and wind smacked against his face as he crunched a path through the snow. The blizzard grew stronger and sleet trickled down the inside of his boots, soaking his socks. His legs would no longer cooperate, his ears were cold and numb, and the temptation to turn around was growing stronger with each step.

Something was wrong. Even though Charles knew the streets of Colchester very well, he now stood in the snow completely lost. Stumbling down Artillery Street, he entered an old Primitive Methodist church for shelter.

Only a dozen people were scattered through the pews. Most of the congregation was snowed in. Charles sat down and waited for the sermon. A thin shoemaker who did not appear to be well-dressed or well-spoken took to the pulpit to preach.

"Our text is found in Isaiah 45:22. 'Look unto me, and be ye saved, all the ends of the earth.'"

Perhaps there is a glimmer of hope for me after all, Charles thought.

The shoemaker continued. "This is a very simple text indeed. It says, 'Look.' Now lookin' don't take a deal of pain. It ain't liftin' your foot or your finger; it is just 'Look.' Well, a man needn't go to college to learn to look. You may be the biggest fool and yet you can look. A man needn't be worth a thousand pounds a year to look. Anyone can look; even a child can look."

The shoemaker looked at Charles. "Young man, you look miserable!"

Charles gasped. It was certainly true, but he wasn't accustomed to being told so from the pulpit.

"And you will always be miserable," the shoemaker hollered, "unless you obey my text! Look unto me, I am sweatin' great drops of blood. Look unto me; I am hangin' on the cross. Look unto me; I am dead and buried. Look unto me; I rise again. Look unto me; I ascend to heaven. Look unto me; I am sitting at the Father's right hand. O poor sinner, look unto me! Look unto me!"

Charles did not remember much more of the shoemaker's sermon; he was too possessed with the one thought: "Look unto me." They were the words he needed to hear, and for the first time in his life, Charles Haddon Spurgeon, later to become the prince of preachers, looked to Jesus.

"I looked," he later said, "until I could almost have looked my eyes away."[1]

River Lark, Isleham, England, 2002

A word of wisdom—if you take a pilgrimage to the Lark River to see the spot where Spurgeon was baptized, be sure to wear thick jeans, thick socks and even thicker boots. I learned this lesson the hard way. In flip-flops, shorts and a T-shirt, I trudged through the overgrown weeds, kicking myself along the way for thinking that hot British weather demanded beach attire.

Next to Jesus and my dad, Charles Haddon Spurgeon is my hero. I would sell the shirt off my back to buy one of his books. I began reading him as a teenager when I discovered that he, too, had a passion for *Pilgrim's Progress*, which he read over a hundred times. Though Spurgeon lived on the other side of the Atlantic and died well over a century ago, when I read his sermons and prayers, the seams of my soul are loosened and hints of heaven slip inside.

After his conversion in the Primitive Methodist church, Spurgeon began to preach the gospel throughout Cambridgeshire. His vocal talent, expert grasp of the Scriptures and dedication to simple explanation of the gospel sparked revival in the heart of England during a time of scripted pulpit performances and expository absence. Though he was only in his early twenties and lacked any formal theological training, Spurgeon's popularity spread across England, and he became known as the "boy preacher of the fens."

Without the aid of microphones or amplifiers, Spurgeon preached to crowds of more than twenty-three thousand people, a feat reminiscent of George Whitefield and John Wesley a hundred years prior. The bulk of Spurgeon's ministry, however, occurred in London as pastor of the Metropolitan Tabernacle, a church seating approximately six thousand. Spurgeon was megachurch before the megachurch existed, and he knew the name of every member in his congregation (and most of their pets' names too). With great clarity he communicated the truths of the Scriptures in a language earthy and easy to digest. Rumor has it that Queen Victoria even disguised herself as a peasant woman and snuck into the Metropolitan Tabernacle to hear him.

A pilgrimage to Spurgeon country was a dream come true for me. Since *Pilgrim's Progress* was such a staple for Spurgeon, my father, David and I began our journey in Bedford, England, where John Bunyan composed his famous Christian allegory. One of Spurgeon's ancestors, Job Spurgeon, lived at the same time as Bunyan and was also imprisoned for preaching the gospel without a license. Bunyan's prison no longer stands, but there is a fine museum that contains pictures of Bedford during the time of his imprisonment, a replica of his cell and some early editions of *Pilgrim's Progress*.

We followed Spurgeon's trail in England from Kelvedon where he was born, to Stambourne where he lived with his grandparents, to Colchester where he was converted, to Isleham where he was baptized, to Cambridge where he studied, to Teversham where he preached, to Waterbeach where he pastored, and to London where he served two churches. Needless to say, we were out of breath by the end of it all.

The weeds around the Lark River rose above my shoulders. Our map wasn't drawn to scale, and I checked it again. "I think we're headed in the right direction," I said without a great deal of confidence. My father, David and I continued to walk beside the river, avoiding painful thistles. We were looking for a small stone plaque in the ground that marked the exact location of Spurgeon's baptism, but our expedition had led us into a jungle of angry plants snagging at our legs and pulling at our clothes. They seemed to be warning us to stay away.

"The last time I was here," my father said, "it wasn't nearly this overgrown."

I carefully unwrapped a vine of thorns that was sucking on my leg and took another step toward the river. "I'll go on from here," I said. "There's no need for all three of us to get lost looking for this plaque." They agreed.

From where I was standing I could almost see the water's edge. Its quiet gushing was close, and I knew Spurgeon's plaque was located somewhere on its banks. I had to go farther. Step by step I inched through the messy marsh. Carnivorous plants scratched me, taunting and tearing. I almost expected to see the skeletons of other pilgrims who had tried to reach Spurgeon's plaque but instead were itched into an early grave. I blazed along furiously despite the green aggression. I was a determined pilgrim, and if it was war they wanted, by George, it was war they were going to get!

More than a century earlier Charles Haddon Spurgeon had stepped into the icy Isleham stream. Gusts of wind cut ripples through the water, and the current almost swept him off his feet. But Charles had not turned back. As a baby he had been baptized in the Presbyterian church, but this fish wanted to swim in the waters of baptism himself as a symbol of his new life in Christ. A small crowd watched as he waded toward the preacher in the water. In his own words, "I felt as if heaven and earth and hell might all gaze upon me, for I was not ashamed, then and there, to own myself a follower of the Lamb. My timidity was washed away; it floated down the river into the sea, and must have been devoured by the fishes, for I have never felt anything of the kind since."[2]

Charles came up out of the water proud to have publicly professed his dedication to Christ. His outward ministry had begun, and it was only a matter of time before his extemporaneous wit, natural charm and devotion to the doctrines of the faith would challenge the spiritual stagnation accumulating in England and bring feeling once again to the numbed body of Christ.

I longed for numbness as I plowed through the thorny plants. Even more, I wanted a chainsaw, some gasoline and a set of strike-anywhere matches. Twenty minutes had passed since I departed from my group, and I was deep in enemy territory. I stopped to breathe. "Okay," I said, trying to be logical, "if I were going to be baptized again, where would I do it?" I reached down to smack some godforsaken creature off my leg. "Certainly not in this river," I muttered, wiping bug blood and brains off my body. I soon realized it was useless. A giant insect leeched onto my ankle, and I must have jumped for five minutes before forcing myself to retreat to the safety of civilization. How embarrassing.

By the time I reached the group, I had already committed to return to this river when all the malicious plants had been mowed away. I considered taking a torch to the whole place then and there, but we had many miles to drive and other sites to see. Defeat tasted sour on my tongue, but as we drove away I looked back through the window and mouthed the wise words of Arnold Schwarzenegger: "I'll be back."

A PILGRIM'S PERSPECTIVE

Pilgrimage benefits the believer in many ways, but above all it gives us perspective on God, faith and how we encounter both. Tom Wright defines the pilgrim as "someone who goes on a journey in the hope of encountering God, or meeting him in a new way."[3] I have found that the process of pilgrimage is more transformative than simply reaching a destination. Each step of the journey involves deeper communion with God, and by the end of it, we discover that we have encountered him thousands of times along the way.

In the movie *Napoleon Dynamite,* Pedro tells the student body of his high school, "Vote for me, and all your wildest dreams will come true." Two thousand years before that, a man named Jesus stood before similar crowds and promised the exact opposite: "If anyone would come after me, he must deny himself and take up his cross daily and follow me" (Luke 9:23). What a thing to say! Speeches like that don't win popularity contests. In fact, following Jesus turned the disciples' wildest dreams into their darkest nightmares, and every one of them was persecuted.

But there is another side of the coin. Jesus goes on to say, "For whoever wants to save his life will lose it, but whoever loses his life for me will save it" (Luke 9:24). This is a tricky paradox indeed. Being a Christian isn't popular, especially in a pluralistic society, but the cost of following Christ pales in comparison to the benefits of gaining eternal life. Christ's disciples developed a pilgrim's perspective that looked through the thorns and weeds of this world to another life, another birth and another home.

The thief on the cross had looked over his shoulder a thousand times. We don't know what put him on the cross. He might have stolen something expensive from someone important, or he might have stolen something inexpensive from someone unimportant. We do not know his fault, only his fate. And when we meet him in the twenty-third chapter of Luke, he is paying for his crimes with his life.

Hanging beside him was another criminal. The plaque above his head read, "King of the Jews." He was a king who never harmed, cheated or robbed anyone. He never lied or cursed or gossiped. When Jesus was hungry, he did not steal. When he was angry, he did not swear. His words were kind. His possessions were few. He even paid taxes to Caesar. And yet there he was, hanging on a cross, dying the death of a criminal.

The thief beside him was close to death and his eyes were slowly shutting. But before he died, he stole one last thing—a look. It was a little look, a passing peek, a split-second stare, but within that look there was enough salvation to last him for all eternity. Spurgeon says:

Recollect, too, that at that moment when the thief believed in Christ, all the disciples had forsaken Him and fled. John might be lingering at a little distance, and holy women may have stood further off, but no one was present to bravely champion the dying Christ. Judas had sold Him, Peter had denied Him, and the rest had forsaken Him; and it was then that the dying thief called Him "Lord" and said, "Remember me when you come into your kingdom."[4]

Charles Spurgeon looked to God in a wooden pew; the thief on the cross looked to God on a wooden cross. Spurgeon found God at the beginning of his earthly pilgrimage; the thief on the cross found him at its end. Nevertheless, with Christ as their commonality, they both were given access into eternity.

The last year of Spurgeon's earthly existence was marked with extreme bouts of gout and depression. Influenza had besieged his body, and at the age of fifty-seven, he climbed the stairs of his pulpit for the last time. He had preached the gospel for forty years, and he knew his pilgrimage was coming to a close. His wife, Susannah, and several of his closest friends went with him to the sunny resort he often frequented in Mentone, France. Little did he know it would be the last time. The first letter he sent back to London reflected an improving health, but his condition quickly worsened. After writing a letter of encouragement to the prince of Wales concerning the loss of his son, the prince of preachers slipped into a coma.

On January 1, 1892, Charles Haddon Spurgeon blinked and breathed his last. In the final moments of his life, Susannah was at his side. She held his hand and heard the last words from his lips: "Oh wifey, I have had such a blessed time with my Lord. My work is done. I have fought the good fight. I have finished my course. I have kept the faith."[5] At five minutes past eleven, the pilgrim went home.

A telegraph was sent around the world to spread the news of his death. People from Asia to Australia to America mourned the loss. The great American preacher and educator B. H. Carroll said, "Last Sunday night at Mentone, France, there died the greatest man of modern times. If every crowned head in Europe had died that night, the event would not be so momentous as the death of this one man."[6] No longer could cold winters plague him or sicknesses assail him. No longer could the routines of life distract him from the gaze of God. Spurgeon's bags were packed and his passport stamped. All that remained was the journey home. And the Christ he loved so dearly and taught so clearly was at last before his eyes.

When God is at the center of our lives, our lives are finally centered. When he occupies our thoughts, feelings, motives and passions his desires become our wildest dreams. We are his wicks, and when he dips us into the wax of his will we burn like beacons in a dark and dreary land. He replaces our burdens with blessings, our sorrows with sweetness and our troubles with triumphs. We love him for it. Death no longer scares us, life becomes worth living, and one morning we get out of bed and discover that our wildest dreams really have come true. Jesus, our dream, is ours. The trivial things we once enjoyed are eclipsed by the beauty of his presence, and nothing can separate us from the life we have in Jesus Christ.

Lord, we are not what we want to be. This is our sorrow. Oh, that you would, by your Spirit, help us in the walks of life to adorn the doctrine of God our Savior in all things. . . . May his joy be in us, for then only can our joy be full.

CHARLES HADDON SPURGEON

AMAZING GRACE

The Secret of Silence

I am not what I ought to be,
I am not what I want to be,
I am not what I hope to be,
But by the grace of God
I am not what I was.

JOHN NEWTON

North Atlantic Ocean, East of Newfoundland, March 21, 1748
Salt water rushed into John Newton's cabin, waking him from a deep sleep. Gale-force winds and punishing waves tore holes in the timber planks of the ship, threatening to sink her at any moment. The Greyhound had proven herself a seaworthy vessel, but the seven-thousand-mile journey from the west coast of Africa to the southern banks of Newfoundland via the east coast of Brazil had taken its toll. The ocean had already claimed some of the crew and most of the cargo, but the stubborn boat remained afloat. John Newton dashed out of his cabin and climbed onto the deck as his whole life flashed before his eyes.

It had been a short life so far—only twenty-two years in all. Born in Wapping, London (close to the Tower of London), on July 24, 1725, John Newton was the son of a merchant ship commander who often sailed the Mediterranean Sea. When John was eleven, his father introduced him to the business of shipping and even took his son on six ocean voyages before his retirement. His mother, on the other hand, had nothing to do with the water. She was a frail, inward-looking woman who nurtured John's spiritual life by teaching him Scripture verses in hopes that one day he would become a preacher.

In 1744, England and France were on the brink of war and the British navy needed fresh sailors. John Newton was forcibly enlisted and became a midshipman on the Harwich. Unable to bear the harsh conditions, he escaped, but he was soon recaptured, publicly flogged and demoted. After much debate, John was commissioned to a slave ship bound for the coast of Sierra Leone, Africa. After six months of collecting slaves along the African coast, the captain suddenly died. A new opportunity arose for John, and it was agreed that he would live and work in Africa as the servant of a wealthy English slave trader.

John Newton admired his master's occupation and eventually adopted it as his own, carrying slaves across the Atlantic Ocean to sell them in the New World. Slavery had been practiced in Africa long before the Europeans arrived, and Newton often bought his slaves from African tribe leaders who had taken their slaves from defeated rival tribes. Newton later disapproved of the inhumane practice of slavery, and after convincing William Wilberforce to join his cause, both men became leading figures in the abolitionist movement.

But while John was still living in Africa, he developed malaria and was cruelly mistreated by the English trader's African mistress. She verbally assailed him, threw rocks at him, mocked and ridiculed him, and fed him so meagerly that in a letter he wrote home to Mary Catlett, the girl he would one day marry, he said, "Sometimes I have not had half a good meal in the course of a month."[1] He would have starved to death were it not for the kindness of the slaves who secretly shared their own morsels with him, not to mention the cassava roots behind his hut that he dug up and ate during the night. It seemed the prodigal son had landed in his pigpen, but it would still be a long while before he came to his senses.

In 1748, John's father heard of his son's terrible predicament and arranged for help. John was located and rescued by Anthony Gother, captain of the Greyhound, a ship that traded gold, ivory, dyers wood and beeswax. While on board, Newton took up cursing and drinking. He despised Christianity and acted so profanely that even the hardened sailors were shocked. Oddly enough, Newton discovered an English translation of Thomas à Kempis's *Imitation of Christ,* a book written for monks in the fifteenth century about the teachings of Christ. As he pored over its pages, a question kept surfacing in his mind: *What if all these things are true?*

It was a question Newton could not now ignore as the violent waves of the Atlantic Ocean swept across the tattered deck of the Greyhound. For hours, John and the crewmen bucketed water out of the boat. "I dreaded death," Newton recounts, "and my heart foreboded the worst, if the Scriptures, which I had long since opposed, were true."[2] Eventually the wind subsided and the crewmen nailed their clothes to the interior of the ship, patching what the sea had forcefully opened. A ship carrying ordinary cargo would have already sunk, but beeswax and wood, which are lighter than water, filled the compartments of the Greyhound and prevented a total submersion. Deep contemplation and disappointment marked the following weeks. The wind was against them, their rations were running out, and they began to fear the worst—cannibalism.

Suddenly, as if from the very mouth of God, the wind began to blow. The crew spotted Tory Island off the northern coast of Ireland, and they anchored in the town of Lough Swill. Newton recounts the moment: "About this time I began to know that there is a God who hears and answers prayer,"[3] and for the remainder of his life, John Newton celebrated that unforgettable event when God saved him from the depths of the sea. He had been shown amazing grace, and after becoming a preacher in Olney, England, he wrote, "Through many dangers toils and snares I have already come; 'tis grace has brought me safe thus far, and grace will lead me home."

Fresh Air Farm, Birmingham, Alabama, January 2001

It was the cheapest pilgrimage of my life: only eleven dollars, including gas—though for a poor college kid, this was big bucks. Our university offered a religion elective class on Christian spirituality led by professor Dennis Sansom. It was a class that challenged me to explore the inner dimensions of the spiritual life and engage the ancient disciplines of the Christian faith. At the end of the course, as our final project in spiritual discipline, our class took a field trip to the Fresh Air Farm, a spiritual retreat located on the top of a beautiful mountain.

The rules were simple. For one day and one night we would read, fast, pray and sleep, but at no time were we allowed to say a single word. We could roam where we wanted, write what we wanted or sit next to anyone we pleased, but in doing these activities we had to remain absolutely quiet. We were pilgrims pursuing the art of sacred silence and, I must say, it was a rough road to travel.

The early desert fathers believed that "to be on pilgrimage is to be silent" *(peregrinatio est tacere).*[4] One of them, Abbot Agatho, even carried a stone in his mouth for three years until he learned to be silent.[5] The closest thing to this I had ever experienced was wearing braces, but unfortunately braces made me scream more than they made me silent.

There I sat. No cell phone to talk on. No music to listen to. No television to watch. The small garden surrounding me offered little entertainment except for the chirping crickets that made me sorely jealous. Occasionally a classmate would walk by, and it gave me unexpected joy to know that he or she, too, was struggling to keep lips stitched.

Why was such an easy task so difficult? Why was the discipline of silence so demanding on my soul? This was not rocket science, metaphysics or calculus. It demanded no energy, imagination or creativity. And yet, as I sat by myself in the stillness of that garden, something inside me resisted the quiet; if a little spider had suddenly sneezed, I would have suffered unbearable anguish not to say, "God bless you!"

Birmingham has been my home for the past eighteen years. While many people call it the "Magic City," history books remember it as a racist city. Founded after the Civil War in 1871, Birmingham became an eighteenth-century industrial enterprise, producing enormous amounts of steel from its coal, iron ore and limestone deposits. During the 1960s, however, the eyes of the world watched as tensions escalated between blacks and whites and violence inevitably broke out.

The city was nicknamed "Bombingham" because of the eighteen un-solved bombings in black neighborhoods, along with the notorious bomb-ing of the Sixteenth Street Baptist Church by the Ku Klux Klan that killed four young girls and injured twenty-two other members of the congrega-tion. In April of 1963, civil rights leader Martin Luther King Jr. was im-prisoned in the Birmingham jail. On scraps of toilet paper and in newspa-per margins, he wrote a letter to his white fellow clergymen hoping that "the dark clouds of racial prejudice will soon pass away."[6] Standing on the shoulders of John Newton and William Wilberforce, Dr. King fought for racial reconciliation and advocated peaceful demonstrations. "In the end," King said, "we will remember not the words of our enemies, but the silence of our friends."[7]

On top of a mountain overlooking this sin-scarred city, I struggled to maintain my own silence. My quiet retreat became a silent protest—not against racial segregation but against inward segregation. The chatty nature of my life had separated me from God, and my world had become too noisy for me to notice him. So numb was I to the voice of God that even when I prayed, lingering commercials, talk shows and music videos completely consumed me.

Our culture is scared of silence. The first thing I do when I enter a hotel room is turn on the television to escape the haunting quiet. Henri Nouwen suggests that "for most people, silence creates itchiness and nervousness. Many experience silence not as full and rich, but as empty and hollow. For them silence is like a gaping abyss which can swallow them up."[8] We see this paralyzing fear of silence in our workplaces, at our dinner tables and even on our television shows, where producers fear nothing more than dead air.

Silence goes against our grain. We are creatures of conversation. Ever since God created us with the spoken word, we have not stopped talking. At the Tower of Babel, God splintered our spoken language, but even today we still babble against him with our words. According to Solomon, "When words are many, sin is not absent, / but he who holds his tongue is wise" (Proverbs 10:19). In many ways, the absence of words prepares us for conversation with Christ.

As I went to bed that night, having said nothing since I arrived at the Fresh Air Farm, I realized that there are two kinds of people in this world: amplifiers and antennas. As a recovering amplifier, I can say from experience that I enjoy producing lots of noise. Put me in a crowd of people and let me go. This is why silence comes hard for me.

But silence helps us to be more like antennas, ready to receive any signal the Savior needs to send us. My urge to be an amplifier is strong, and I when I woke up the next morning, I felt it more than ever. But after a day and night of wordless meditation and inward contemplation, I came to understand why God insisted that we "be still and know that I am God" (Psalm 46:10).

The next morning, I spent a good portion of an hour and three cups of tea pondering the relationship between knowing and going. Pilgrims are called to go where God leads them, but they are also called to know that God is going before them. The motivation for going is built on the foundation of knowing. This is why Paul refuses to let us walk by sight, because at best we see as through a glass darkly. Rather, it is faith that leads us, faith that guides us, and faith that shows us the way.

Before David's life raged with the rapids of adultery and homicide, God led him beside quiet waters. While the Philistine giant taunted Israel, God met David beside the river, seeming to say, "David, there are many rocks you could use for this battle. You could pick up a jagged stone that would puncture Goliath's skin, or you could pick up a sandstone that might explode like a grenade. But David, I want you to choose five smooth stones— stones that have been shaped and smoothed by the calm, quiet water rushing over them."

Silent moments with the Savior season us for spiritual combat. Our journey through life is so splashy with activity that we often struggle just to keep our heads above the waves. Henri Nouwen submits, "We have, indeed, to fashion our own desert where we can withdraw every day, shake off our compulsions, and dwell in the gentle healing presence of our Lord."[9] No matter where we are or what we are doing, we can always take a moment to be with our Maker—morning moments, shower moments, stoplight moments, lunchtime moments, midnight moments. When Christians spend time with the Living Water while being led by streams of quiet water, they will become smooth enough to travel through the air when God pulls them from his pocket.

Jesus went to the quiet water to find a rock named Simon. Simon had grown up with the sea—swimming through it, fishing from it, bathing in it. And when we meet him floating in a boat in Luke 5, he is right at home on the waves.

The hours had come and gone without a single fish. Make no mistake, Simon and his friends were fine fishermen. They knew exactly where to steer the boat and how to throw the nets, but something else was attracting the attention of the fish.

"Try throwing your nets on the other side of the boat," a stranger said, standing on the shore.

Simon laughed. "On the other side of the boat? You must not be from around here. We've cast our nets into every nook and cranny of this sea! The fish are ignoring us today."

"I'll have a talk with the fish," the stranger said. "They might ignore you, but they cannot ignore the God who gave them their gills."

And when Simon obeyed the stranger, the boat almost flipped over from all the flopping. After a day of stillness and achieving nothing, in the quiet water Simon met a stranger who changed his life forever. Jesus carved a new name on his tackle box that day—Peter (*Petros*), the Greek word for "rock." And what a dent he made in the devil's forehead.

Not long after my pilgrimage to the Fresh Air Farm, I found myself

searching the aisles of a music store for a jazz CD. I wanted Miles Davis, The-
lonious Monk or George Gershwin. At last I found one. Seventeen dollars
and ninety-five cents seemed a bit steep, but I bought it anyway. As I got into
my car, I peeled off the plastic wrapping and shoved the new CD into the
player. I waited. Silence. No music, no noise, no nothing. "This isn't happening," I said, skipping to tracks number two, three and four. I pulled the CD
out and examined it. An enormous scratch ran from the top of the disk to
the bottom. Perhaps I accidentally scratched it after opening it. Or perhaps
it was already scratched when I bought it. Whatever the case, I tried to play
it again, but no sound came out; it just played silence. As the green light
blinked to red, I sat in silence, forced to deal with my frustration. Having
just taken a spiritual retreat, I wasn't feeling very spiritual.

The light changed again and I sped off, angry at the turn of events. But
while I was driving, a thought interrupted my irritation. Perhaps this CD
could help me break my addiction to noise. I turned up the volume. Loud,
blaring nothing burst through my speakers, and I listened attentively to it.
The quiet noise was eerie, but I began to appreciate it. I began to understand
what Barbara Brown Taylor meant when she said, "It takes thousands of
words, coming at us every moment, to distract us from the terrible silence
within."[10] As I drove along that road, track after empty track, mile after quiet
mile, I discovered that the terrible silence became a tolerable silence, and
then, dare I even say it, a treasured silence.

I never returned that CD. Seventeen dollars and ninety-five cents was a
lot to pay for a broken record, but for a good lesson on silence, it was a bar-
gain. From time to time, I'll hit the play button on that broken CD. Noise
never comes out, but I listen to it anyway. It helps me focus on God and reminds me that there is a secret to silence—active listening.

A year later, after I graduated from college, I worked at a piano store in
Birmingham. For hours I sat in long periods of silence between customer
checkouts. It gave me time to think about the things in life that really matter. Things like faith, theology and, most importantly, my beautiful new
bride, Rebecca.

But one day while I was in the middle of my thoughts, a familiar melody broke the silence. It was a melody infused with history—"Amazing Grace." I thought of John Newton and his struggles with the slave industry. I thought of Dr. King and his dream of racial reconciliation and equality. And as the piano player tickled those ivories, one after another, up and down the piano, I realized that the white keys need the black keys just as much as the black keys need the white keys. And if God were ever going to play his holy music in our land, it would seem right for him to use us both.

PREACHING TO THE PEWS

Some things in life are unforgettable. The tune of the ice cream truck driving down a hot summer street. The smell of freshly cut grass scattered on a soccer field. The sweet sigh of relief that comes after finishing a long exam in college. These are memories we will take with us to our graves.

Silence must minister to us before we can minister to others, and I'll never forget the silence of the pews, the empty, barren pews of my college campus chapel. I would escape there from time to time to be alone with God. When all the classes had ended for the day and most students were sleeping, studying or partying, I walked there. It was only a five-minute journey, a short pilgrimage, but it was a place of spiritual retreat for me. It was a place of silence. Along the way I would pass one or two people, but for the most part, it was just me and Jesus walking to the church in the shadows.

The college environment does not always promote silence and solitude, so I had to steal it. I had to carve my quiet from the marble of university life. With a Bible in one hand and a newly written sermon in the other, I crept through the chapel door hoping no one would see me. Stained-glass windows towered over my head as I snuck down the center aisle. Like a sailor climbing up the front of a wooden ship, I inched my way into the pulpit. I was still a very green preacher and my stomach churned with seasickness when I had to prepare my sermons. But I had one rule: If I were going to preach before people on the weekend, I was certainly going to practice before angels during the week.

Often I preach in small rural churches throughout Alabama. Many of these churches have not yet been influenced by the civil rights movement. Occasionally I'll discover a congregation that still retains their prejudices, and I'll think of John Newton and his fight against slavery. I'll think of Martin Luther King Jr. and all the work he did to create an environment of equality among Americans. Sometimes, when I'm preaching in the remote hills of my beloved state, God changes my heart before I take to the pulpit and has me preach the gospel through the lenses of racial reconciliation.

So there I stood, waiting for God to finish introducing me so I could begin. I looked across the silent pews. The eight-page handwritten sermon intimidated me, but the silence was soothing. It did not matter how many words I would mispronounce or how bad my eye contact was. The whole chapel was pitch dark and there was plenty of room for mistakes. I opened my mouth to preach, knowing that my sermons were usually longer than the demons wanted and shorter than the angels wanted, but neither would complain. After closing the service with a quick prayer and a quicker invitation, I walked back to my room, having been comforted by the midnight silence, ready to speak the words of God to the people of God.

Late have I loved you,
Beauty so ancient and so new,
Late have I loved you.
Lo, you were within, but I outside,
Seeking there for you. . . .
You called, shouted, broke through my deafness;
You flared, blazed, banished my blindness;
You lavished your fragrance, I gasped,
And now I pant for you; I tasted you touched me,
And I burned for your peace.

SAINT AUGUSTINE

FROM SUNSHINE TO SHADOW

The Cost of Discipleship

I believe in the sun though it is late in rising.
I believe in love though it is absent.
I believe in God though He is silent.

UNSIGNED INSCRIPTION IN A CAVE NEAR COLOGNE,
WHERE JEWS HAD BEEN HIDING

Flossenbürg Death Camp, Germany, April 9, 1945
Six o'clock came early for Dietrich Bonhoeffer—early in the morning and early in his life. He was only thirty-nine years old, but the Zossen papers had been discovered, Bonhoeffer's closest friends had been arrested, and his involvement in the plot to assassinate Adolf Hitler had been exposed. All that remained of the sunshine was the shadows.

Born in 1906 in Breslau, Germany, Dietrich was raised to love the arts. By the age of ten he painted, sculpted and even played Mozart's sonatas on the piano. Books became his friends, and he loved to read great adventure stories like *Pinocchio*, *Heroes of Everyday*, and a German translation of *Uncle Tom's Cabin*. Later in his life, when he sat tormented in a six-foot-by-nine-foot prison cell, the memory of these childhood stories would bring him much comfort.

His love for God and his passion for books drove him to study theology at the University of Tübingen. He was only sixteen years old, but people thought he was much older. He joined a fraternity called the Hedgehog and quickly earned a reputation for being able to defend his thoughts with vigor and clarity.

In the spring of 1924, Bonhoeffer took a pilgrimage to Rome. Fascinated by Roman art and architecture, he explored the city with great excitement, eating Italian cheese by the Trevi Fountain, visiting the church of Santa Maria Maggiore and participating in a morning mass at Saint Peter's Basilica. Since he was away from his studies in Germany, Bonhoeffer spent long periods of time contemplating the great questions of life: "How can we better understand God?" "How can Christians live in society?" "What does it mean to live ethically?" His quest for these answers would shape him into one of the greatest theologians and Christian thinkers of the twentieth century.

In 1933, Adolf Hitler rose to power and the Nazi regime shadowed the German landscape. Bonhoeffer, who preached in Berlin and taught at the university, spoke boldly against the Nazi empire. When Hitler introduced the Aryan Clause, which banned Jews from civil service jobs, Bonhoeffer's stance against the government solidified and he wrote a paper called "The Church and the Jewish Question." In this paper, he urged the church to first require the state to answer for its actions; second, to embrace those who were suffering as victims; and third, "not just to bandage the victims under the wheel, but to jam a spoke in the wheel itself."[1]

Against the background of war, pain, suffering and death, Bonhoeffer became a spoke that threatened to rattle the wheel. He was involved in several attempts to take Hitler's life, but none came to fruition. On April 5, 1943, two months after proposing to Maria von Wedemeyer, Bonhoeffer was arrested and taken to Tegel prison. He was later transferred to a Gestapo prison, to Buchenwald and eventually to the death camp of Flossenbürg.

On July 20, 1944, a suitcase containing a time bomb was placed next to Hitler at Wolfschanze, three hundred miles from Berlin. Bonhoeffer had participated in this plot, and if successful, he would have been released from prison and all the charges against him would have been dropped. Hopes were high that this bomb would end a regime responsible for the deaths of millions of innocent people. When the bomb exploded at 12:50 p.m., four people were killed and many more were burned. When the smoke cleared, however, Adolf Hitler remained alive. An estimated seven thousand people were arrested in connection to this assassination attempt, and even though Bonhoeffer was imprisoned at the Tegel prison when it happened, the Zossen papers that bound him to the conspiracy were discovered. Hitler immediately sent personal orders for his death.

At six o'clock in the morning, just before his death at Flossenbürg, Bonhoeffer knelt down to pray. The reality of prison life had overshadowed the dream of married life, and Bonhoeffer's stance against the evils of the Nazi regime would cost him his life. The prison doctor witnessed Bonhoeffer's final moments. "I was most deeply moved by the way this lovable man prayed, so devout and so certain that God heard his prayer."[2] Bonhoeffer was brave and composed as he climbed the stairs of the gallows, and on the morning of April 9, 1945, Dietrich Bonhoeffer was hung.

His life was taken, but Bonhoeffer's words did not die. Through his writings and letters, we get a glimpse of his theology and passionate devotion to the Christian life. Of primary importance to Bonhoeffer was the costliness of Christianity. In his book *The Cost of Discipleship*, he explains that grace should cost us something. He did not mean that grace is earned, nor did he insist that Christians seek the path of suffering; rather, Bonhoeffer realized that a Christian's actions and attitudes reflect a nature not understood by the world and, "if they persecuted me," Jesus said, "they will persecute you also" (John 15:20).

Bonhoeffer differentiates between cheap grace and costly grace. Cheap grace wants the best of both worlds—the world of sin and the world of salvation. He argues that grace without a price is not grace at all. In his own words:

> Cheap grace is the preaching of forgiveness without requiring repentance, baptism without Church discipline, Communion without confession, absolution without contrition. Cheap grace is grace without

discipleship, grace without the Cross, grace without Jesus Christ, living and incarnate.[3]

Costly grace, on the other hand, "is costly because it calls us to follow, and it is grace because it calls us to follow Jesus Christ. It is costly because it costs a man his life, and it is grace because it gives a man the only true life."[4] Bonhoeffer believed that a Christ who does not change us does not save us.

With his life and death, Dietrich Bonhoeffer exemplified the cost of discipleship. In a memorial service for him broadcast over British radio, Bishop Bell said, "Where he went and whoever he spoke with—whether young or old—he was fearless, regardless of himself, and with it all, devoted heart and soul to his parents, his friends, his country as God willed it to be, to his Church and to his Master."[5] It has been more than fifty years since his death, but Bonhoeffer's legacy of courage and faith continues to exist in the hearts and minds of all those who proclaim the truth of God's love to a world of pain, suffering and disillusionment.

Buchenwald, Germany, 1996

My stomach was queasy, but I could not look away. Bodies, hundreds of them, piled one on top of the other. Some were children, others older. Some were clothed, others naked. Together, their ghostly faces cried out from the picture, begging me to remember them and promising to haunt me if I ever forgot. I have not forgotten. I walked down the halls of the concentration camp museum in Buchenwald heartbroken, angry and impotent to help them. "How could anyone let this happen?" I asked, tearing myself from one gory picture only to fix my eyes on another.

Our pilgrimage through Germany lasted three weeks, and we did not want to go home before exploring the concentration camps of Dachau and Buchenwald, where the cruelty and brutality of the Nazi regime manifested itself so powerfully. We arrived by train in the city of Weimar and checked into the Elephant Hotel, which Hitler himself frequented. The city of Weimar has been a pilgrimage site for many German intellectuals because it was the home of poet, playwright and novelist Johann Wolfgang von Goethe, who embodied German enlightenment in the eighteenth century. The city houses art galleries, museums and a German theater.

The concentration camp of Buchenwald was one of the first and largest of Nazi concentration camps. The name Buchenwald is German for "beech forest" because the camp itself is located deep in the woods, about eight kilometers from Weimar. Goethe often walked through these woods, receiving inspiration and creativity from their beauty. But the camp that lay before our eyes was anything but beautiful.

Its gatehouse has changed little since the first male prisoners walked through its doors in July 1937 and female prisoners in 1944. An inscription on the gate remains: *Jedem Das Seine* (To Each His Own). Prisoners were stripped of their clothes, bathed and taken to their quarters at the north end of the camp. The south end was reserved for the guard barracks and the administrative buildings that remain today, though they were heavily damaged in a bombing attack on August 24, 1944. A zoo was even built for the guards and their families, and its bear pit has been preserved. Near one of the barracks stood the "Goethe tree" where the poet sometimes visited. Although it no longer stands, its stump can still be seen near the storehouse.

We reverently entered the camp, imagining how terrified the prisoners must have been when they arrived from the train station. While not technically an extermination camp like Auschwitz or Flossenbürg, mass killings of Russian POWs, Jews, Christians, gypsies, homosexuals and political enemies did occur within its walls. Slave labor, starvation and medical experiments resulted in the deaths of an estimated fifty-one thousand inmates by 1945. In one medical experiment, 729 prisoners were injected with vaccines for typhus, and 280 of those died from exposure to the bacteria. The inmates were surrounded by watchtowers, electric barbed-wire fences and automatic machine guns that made escape impossible.

Dietrich Bonhoeffer was brought to this camp on February 7, 1945. For almost two months he was imprisoned in the basement of a Nazi guard's barracks. He formed many friendships with political prisoners, including Captain Payne Best who said that "his soul really shone in the dark desperation of our prison."[6] As I walked to the crematorium where thousands of bodies were burned, I thought of Bonhoeffer's famous words: "When Christ calls a man, He bids him come and die."[7]

Was I really prepared to give up my life for my faith? Was Christ that important to me? These questions followed me into the room where several brick ovens lined the wall, bearing witness to the hundreds of bodies that were burned. Where was God while this was happening? Was he deaf to the cries of the inmates? Was he blind to the prisoners' pain? Or perhaps, dare we even think it, was he just silent? Barbara Brown Taylor comments:

> It is no coincidence, I think, that so much of the literature on the silence of God has been written by the Jews. *The Exile of the Word: From the Silence of the Bible to the Silence of Auschwitz* by Andre Neher. *The Disappearance of God* by Richard Elliot Friedman. *In Speech and In Silence: The Jewish Quest for God* by David Wolpe. *The Eclipse of God* by Martin Buber. Each of these writers is a Holocaust survivor, even if he never set foot in a camp. Each writes with the knowledge that the sky can grow dark with smoke from burning human bodies without so much as a whimper from God.[8]

Never have I been so angry with God, so furious that he could allow such an evil thing to happen. I wrestled with my preconceived notion of a loving God, and I struggled with the fact that God allowed his people to suffer cruelly at the hands of Hitler. No doubt Bonhoeffer struggled with these same issues as he stayed in this camp, when smoke from burning bodies rose up into God's nostrils. I knew how God used suffering to teach Job a lesson about his sovereignty, but never before had I seen suffering so explicitly. Never before had I seen human life treated with such single-minded hatred. It just didn't seem fair.

But many things aren't fair. Take the cross, for example. Was it fair of God to punish his son for the sins of his people? Was it fair of Jesus to embrace the nails for crimes committed against both humanity and divinity? I discovered a lot about myself that afternoon. I discovered that I knew very little of Christian suffering. I could not identify with the apostle Paul who said, "I want to know Christ and the power of his resurrection and the fellowship of sharing in his sufferings" (Philippians 3:10).

The Christianity I wanted was a casual Christianity, a cotton-candy faith that melts in the mouth before it sinks to the soul. I wanted a Christianity of health, wealth and happiness that let me "name it and claim it." I wanted a Christianity of jellybeans and Jolly Ranchers, built from bricks of earthly materialism, construed from clay of temporary treasure. I wanted a Christ who was too saccharine to save anyone.

But this pilgrimage taught me that being a Christian pilgrim is about ministering to those who are walking beside us. While I did not have the opportunity to stand up against Hitler as Bonhoeffer did, I do have the opportunity to fight against genocide in Sudan, sex trafficking in Southeast Asia and child slavery throughout the world. These are the holocausts and persecutions of my time, and if I do not fight against them as Jesus would have me do, I am just as guilty as those who are committing these evil acts of hatred.

"I shall have no right," Bonhoeffer once wrote to Reinhold Niebuhr, "to participate in the reconstruction of Christian life in Germany after the war if I do not share the trials of this time with my people."[9] As I touched the rounded iron opening of a furnace where countless bodies had once burned, I prayed that God would forgive me for being insensitive to the sufferings Christians endured in the past and that I would boldly stand up for the cause of those who suffer oppression no matter their religious allegiance.

From the crematorium we walked to the museum and spent the remainder of our time perusing dozens of pictures illustrating the gruesome reality of life and death in the concentration camp. On the way out, I struggled for words to write in the visitors' guestbook. The only words that came to mind were these: "Those who forget history are doomed to repeat it."

On April 11, 1945, two days after Bonhoeffer was killed, the Unites States Army marched into Buchenwald and ended the Nazi reign of terror that had assailed its inmates. For the American soldiers who liberated the camp, the scene was horrific. Hundreds of men were crammed into barracks that only had room for fifty, bodies waiting to be burned were stacked upon one another outside the crematorium, and many were dying from starvation and lack of hygiene. To make matters worse, some even died after the liberation because their stomachs were too small to handle the food the soldiers fed them. The scene was vivid evidence of the grisly evils committed by a ruthless empire.

From Weimar we traveled by train to Berlin to see the bunker where Adolf Hitler committed suicide. The actual bunker cannot be seen, but a simple asphalt driveway marks the spot of his death. We took several walking tours around the city. We saw Williams Memorial Church where Bonhoeffer occasionally attended; it has not been rebuilt since it was bombed during the war. We toured Checkpoint Charlie museum where hundreds of people were smuggled in vehicles through the wall separating East Berlin from West.

Our pilgrimage to Germany had come to an end. But as we journeyed across the Atlantic Ocean, I felt that God had used this pilgrimage to stretch me. Perhaps seeing Buchenwald and reading Bonhoeffer had resensitized me to the seriousness of the Christian faith—a faith that has cost many people their lives. Perhaps it forced me to grapple with the reality of my own mortality and in some way prepared me for that great journey of death. But above all, I think it brought me into a deeper knowledge of the God who promises to eradicate all suffering and wipe every tear from every eye. To that end, I have learned to say with Bonhoeffer, "Who am I? They mock me, these lonely questions of mine. Whoever I am, Thou knowest, Oh God, I am thine!"[10]

A THEOLOGY OF THE VALLEY

Pilgrimage does not only confront suffering on a global and cosmic scale. Sometimes it hits close to home as well. I was a freshman in college, and like most first-year college students, I was enjoying life in the fast lane. I was preoccupied with living on my own, playing ping-pong until the wee hours of the morning and waiting for the girl of my dreams to fall into my arms. It was a new beginning to a bright and sunny season in my life.

Little did I see the shadows hovering on the horizon.

Minutes feel like millennia when you're waiting in the doctor's office. As I flipped through the pages of a sports magazine, I knew that something inside me was wrong. It had been wrong for several months, but the doctor would have to tell me how wrong.

His eyes were heavy and his voice was low; this wasn't his first bad news delivery of the day.

"Tell me straight up, doc. How bad is it?" I didn't want any horseplay or beating around the bush. I needed the meat of the matter.

"You have a bleeding disorder," he said. "It's called ulcerative colitis."

"Ulcerative what?" I asked.

"It's a digestive disease," he continued.

"Okay," I replied. "How do we fix it?"

He looked at me and shook his head. "There's no fixing this disease, Christian. Ulcerative colitis has no cure."

"No cure?" I asked. "This is America; there's a cure for everything."

"I wish that were true," he replied. "The only cure for your disease is to surgically remove your entire colon."

"You've got to be kidding," I said. "That will never be an option."

"I hope you are right," he mumbled, scribbling a handful of prescriptions onto a notepad. "While we don't have a cure for your condition, we do have medicines that might suppress your flare-ups if you take them in large enough doses."

I couldn't believe my ears.

"We don't know why some people get it, what triggers it or how to prevent it. All we know is that millions of Americans are diagnosed with ulcerative colitis, and—I have to be honest with you—your chances of colon cancer are doubled, and many people with your illness face premature death."[11]

I left the doctor's office that day feeling lower than I have ever felt in my life. It was a difficult diagnosis to accept, a pilgrimage I didn't want to take, a valley deeper than I wanted to crawl through. But crawl through it I did, and bleed in it I have. Ulcerative colitis is a disease that inflames the colon. Everything I ate, everything that moved through my body sliced its edges like razor blades through a watermelon. I bled until I could bleed no more. I sang the words, "Why should I feel discouraged, why should the shadows come, why should my heart feel lonely, and long for heaven and home? When Jesus is my portion, my constant friend is he. His eye is on the sparrow and I know he watches me."[12] But many days I didn't feel that God was watching me. All I felt were the early hours of the morning, when Jesus and I were doubled over in pain, sobbing on the bathroom floor.

Many nights have passed when my bathroom has been my bedroom and I have begged God to take this thorn from my flesh. But I am learning that it is more sacred to be held by God than to be healed. Attached to every thorn of pain there is a rose of purpose, and in God's arms of love I hear, "Christian, my grace is sufficient for your sickness."

Good theology, the kind worth having in our heads, grows in the valley. John Calvin, a theologian who suffered from gout, kidney stones, tuberculosis, intestinal parasites, hemorrhoids, blood clots and spastic bowel syndrome, once wrote, "[Illnesses] serve us for medicines to purge us from worldly affections, and retrench what is superfluous in us, and since they are to us the messengers of death, we ought to learn to have one foot raised to take our departure when it shall please God."[13] Pain keeps the pilgrim on the path.

In his sermon "The Awful Grace of God," Beeson Divinity School professor and preacher Dr. Robert Smith Jr. explains that we tend to read the first three verses of Psalm 23 loudly, with authority and boldness:

> The LORD is my Shepherd, I shall not be in want.
>   He makes me lie down in green pastures,
> he leads me beside quiet waters,
>   he restores my soul.
> He guides me in paths of righteousness
>   for his name's sake.

But when we get to the valley in verse four, we whisper:

> Even though I walk
>> through the valley of the shadow of death,
> I will fear no evil,
>> for you are with me;
> your rod and your staff,
>> they comfort me.

Then we loudly pick up again in verse five:

> You prepare a table before me
>> in the presence of my enemies.
> You anoint my head with oil;
>> my cup overflows.
> Surely goodness and love will follow me
>> all the days of my life,
> and I will dwell in the house of the Lord
>> forever.

When we hollow out this psalm, however, we hollow out our faith. At the very core of Christianity is the suffering Savior. When we forget his valley, we neglect our own. When we ignore the reality of his brutality, we diminish the grace that leads us through ours. When we gut the valley of the shadow of death, we gut the gospel of life and peace. A theology of the valley is a necessary ingredient for understanding pilgrimage because the path always sinks to the low places. Eugene Peterson writes, "No sooner do we confidently stride out on the road of faith than we trip on an obstruction and fall to the hard surface, bruising our knees and elbows."[14] And we confess with Jonah, "To the roots of the mountains I sank down; the earth beneath barred me in forever" (Jonah 2:6).

A Christian's journey to God is like a bowl of Chinese soup—sometimes it is sweet, sometimes it is sour. When life is sweet, it is easy to be a Christian. When bills are paid, when dishes are done, when clothes are clean.

But a day will come when the phone rings and the voice on the other end of the line says, "I'm sorry, your son was just in a terrible car accident and did not survive." Or the medical report will come in and the doctor will say, "I'm sorry, there's nothing more we can do for you." Suddenly, the soup sours in our mouths, and with David we walk through the valley of the shadow of death.

The valley of the shadow of death is where a real fear confronts a real faith and requires a real relationship with a real shepherd. A. W. Tozer, a profound Christian thinker and author, said, "We want to be saved, but we insist that Christ do all the dying."[15] Christians are like caterpillars, and if we are to be transformed, we must experience down time, a death time, a tomb time, a cocoon time. But when the morning comes, we emerge from the ashes with wings that we did not have before, and we can finish the song, "I sing because I'm happy, I sing because I'm free. His eye is on the sparrow, and I know he's watching me."

My wife makes the best chocolate cake you have ever tasted in your life. Sometimes I'll watch her work in the kitchen. She'll crack the eggs, slice the butter and pour the sugar into the mix (actually, we use Splenda). "Rebecca," I'll ask, "when's that cake going to be ready to eat?"

"In a little while, sweetheart," she'll reply.

Minutes pass. "How about now?"

"No, it still needs one more ingredient," she'll say.

"Do I need to go to the grocery store?"

"No, Christian," she says, "it just needs to be cooked."

As Christians, we love life's good ingredients—the green pasture, the blue water, the restoration for our souls. These mix well in a believer's batter. But let me suggest that our Christianity is incomplete without the heat of the furnace. It is only in the oven of affliction that real character develops, real faith rises and real theology expands.

A pilgrim's path is seldom smooth. There are plenty of potholes, ditches and valleys along the way. From the moment we set foot on this earth to the moment we are lifted to heaven, interruptions and inconveniences assail us.

Dangers distract us. Problems perplex us. But by his grace and for his glory, God shows us that lilies grow in the valleys, and though we are tempered with tempests, we discover that storms shape us more than drizzles do. It is only in the valley that we appreciate the sunshine.

On Tuesday, April 20, 1999, Cassie Bernall had a decision to make. She needed to finish a homework assignment on *Macbeth* for her English class, so she went to the library. At 11:15 a.m., Eric Harris and Dylan Klebold, fellow students, came into the library and started shooting people with the guns they had brought to school. When they came up to Cassie, they asked her a question: "Do you believe in God?" Cassie paused, and then said, "Yes." According to one student, "She must have been scared, but her voice didn't sound shaky. It was strong."[16] After her confession, one of the boys shot her in the head, killing her instantly.

Cassie Bernall verbalized the deepest matters of her heart, and with one simple word she summarized the entire history of the Christian faith—yes. Yes, I give my life for my faith. Yes, I surrender my all to God. Yes, I look death square in the face and find eternal life. Yes.

Cassie went to school that day a student, but she has become a teacher. Her bold expression of faith teaches us that the God who molds the heart and shapes the mind will comfort us when we announce the gospel in the face of oppression, injustice and ungodliness. She teaches us that we don't have to be a super-Christian to please God, just a faithful one. She teaches us that life is not over when this earthly pilgrimage ends; rather, it is just the beginning. Tertullian said that the blood of the martyrs is the seed of the church, and Cassie Bernall stands in a long line of saints who have paid the ultimate price for their relationship with God. It is a price that Bonhoeffer paid, and it is a price that every one of us is asked to afford. Will we say yes to the call?

Lord, in the daytime stars can be seen from the deepest wells,
And the deeper the wells the brighter thy stars shine;

Let me find thy light in my darkness,
Thy life in my death,
Thy joy in my sorrow,
Thy grace in my sin,
Thy riches in my poverty
Thy glory in my valley.

PURITAN PRAYER

THIN PLACES

Don't Forget Your Map

When in some future time I shall sit in a madly crowded assembly
with music and dancing round me, and the wish arises to retire
into the loneliest loneliness, I shall think of Iona.

MENDELSSOHN

Loch Ness, Scotland, August 22, A.D. 565

As legend has it, Columba and his companions reached the river just as the funeral began.

"What happened here?" Columba asked.

"A local villager was swimming in the River Ness," they said, "and a sea creature savagely attacked him. We heard his screams and tried to rescue him, but it was too late."

To the astonishment of the crowd, one of Columba's friends, Lugne Mocumin, jumped into the river to fetch a boat on the other side. The bystanders on shore watched in horror as the sea creature, unsatisfied with its last meal, quickly pursued the monk. Lugne swam with all his might, but the black body of the monster surrounded him and opened its jaws to devour the swimming saint.

Suddenly, Columba shouted with a loud voice, "Go no further, beast. Do not touch the man. Go back at once!" When he invoked the name of God and made the sign of the cross with his hand, the creature fled in terror "so fast one might have thought it was pulled back with ropes."[1] Lugne swam to the other side of the lake and safely returned with the boat. Both the heathen natives on shore and the monastic brethren with Columba worshiped God for the miracle they had just witnessed. And the sea creature disappeared into the murky water of Loch Ness.

Isle of Iona, Scotland, 2002

Against good reason, I embarked on a journey by myself across the windy hills of Iona. Many a pilgrim has disappeared hiking the island alone, but since Iona is shaped like a kidney bean and is only three miles long, the chances of getting lost, hurt or killed seemed slim. Or so I thought.

My destination was Saint Columba's Bay, located at the southern tip of the island. Beautiful green gemstones called "Saint Columba's tears" are found on its sandy shore. Pilgrims are encouraged to go there and pick up two stones, throwing one of them into the sea as a symbol of something in their lives they wish to leave behind and keeping the other as an emblem of their new commitment to Christ. It was on this tiny cove that Saint Columba landed on May 12, 563.

Columba was born into a royal family on December 7, 521, the great-great-grandson of Niall Naoi Ghiallach, an Irish king of the fifth century. Columba's name sounds different in Hebrew, *Jona*, in Greek, *Peristera*, and in Latin, *Columba;* nevertheless, in all three languages his name means "dove." Because he introduced Christianity to Scotland and northern England during the Middle Ages, history would come to know Columba as the "dove of the church."

In his youth, Columba studied at reputable schools and learned a variety of subjects including art, poetry and language. These tools would later assist him on the isle of Iona in illustrating, copying and adorning Gospel manuscripts. Throughout his early life, Columba grew in wisdom and stature and might have become a great king of Ireland were it not for his calling to become a monk and a priest. After receiving his ordination, he established monasteries in Durrow, Kells and Meath.

Problems arose when Columba copied a Psalter at the scriptorium under Finnian but intended to keep the copy for himself. The dispute between Columba and Finnian eventually led to the battle of Cúl Dreimne on the slopes of Ben Bulben in 561, a battle in which three thousand people were slain. Columba's conscience was so heavy that he set out on a journey to save as many people as he had murdered.

With twelve of his closest friends, Columba set sail from his homeland in an act of penance. He first landed at the Kintyre peninsula on the west coast of Scotland but traveled farther up the coast until he reached Iona. According to legend, sun-worshiping druids were already living on this island, and Columba introduced them to Christianity by implanting a cross within a circle as a way of illustrating the sovereignty of God over the elements of nature. Iona soon became an oasis of Christian spirituality, a center for evangelism and a home base for Columba's mission trips throughout England and Scotland. Columba spent much of his time on Iona teaching, preaching, praying and copying Scripture manuscripts.

Iona is not easily accessible. To get there from the United States, a pilgrim travels by plane, car, bus, ferry and barge. It's not the kind of place you just stumble on, but the travel, I must say, is certainly worth the trouble.

Our pilgrimage through Scotland began in Aberdeen, where we met with David Riker, who was pursuing his Ph.D. at the University of Aberdeen at the time. From Aberdeen we journeyed by car on curvy, narrow roads up the green, balding mountains of the Scottish highlands. After crossing Loch Ness, we visited our friends Donald and Jenny McCrae in Gairloch, where my father preached at their parish church. After several days of traveling we arrived at Oban, where we took a ferry to the island of Mull. A bus shuttled us across Mull to Fionnphort, where we boarded a barge to Iona. A cozy bed-and-breakfast on the eastern side of the island welcomed us, and after catching our breath from the hustle and bustle of traveling, we ate a fine meal at a local Irish restaurant.

The next morning we awoke to a strange and mysterious island. According to ancient Celts, certain geographical locations can be thin—not quite earth, not quite heaven, but a mystical place where the boundaries of time and space blur. As I stepped outside the inn to begin my trek to Saint Columba's Bay, I was inundated with sunshine. It was like the whole island was bathing in a jacuzzi of light. As an artist, I have been trained to paint in all kinds of wavelengths—morning dawn, broad daylight and evening twilight. But as I walked down to the blue sapphire water, I came to understand why the druids might have worshiped the sun here. The light was strange and unfamiliar, provoking me to greet it as something new. Post-enlightenment thinking has exalted the power of rationality over the wanderings of imagination, but perhaps the Celts were right about this island. Perhaps it really is thin.

A road leading across Iona takes the pilgrim to the trail that leads south toward Columba's Bay. With a burden on my back and a destination in my mind, I felt like Christian in *Pilgrim's Progress*. On I went, past the small village, past the high Celtic crosses, past the Benedictine nunnery, past the ancient abbey. When I arrived at the top of the hill, the trail suddenly split.

I paused.

Something deep inside told me to take the left path, but the directions I had in my head were of poor quality and my ability to remember them was even poorer. So to the right I went, headed directly in the wrong direction. Perhaps a compass would have been beneficial, because I ended up spending large amounts of energy climbing grassy sand dunes and throwing rocks into the sea, all the while thinking that in no way did my surroundings look like the pictures I had seen of Columba's Bay. Where were all the pilgrims? And the famous green gemstones? Nevertheless, I pressed on in hopes of reaching the bay by lunchtime.

Legend has it that when Columba first reached Iona, one of his followers, Oran, desired to be buried alive as a living sacrifice to the island. Reluctantly, Columba agreed to the macabre request and put him beneath the earth. Three days passed. When Columba and his monks dug him up, they found Oran alive and well. "There is no such great wonder in death, nor is hell what it has been described," Oran said with a smile. Upon hearing this heresy, Columba ordered his monks to bury him again, saying, "Earth, earth on Oran's eyes, lest he further blab!" Oran received his death wish.

I thought of poor Oran as I sat on a rock inside the cove of Port Ban. Clouds had chilled the Iona air and I shivered, wishing I had brought a fleece. *What could be worse than being buried alive?* I wondered. I shuddered at the thought—confined in a coffin without air, light or mobility. I suppose being eaten by ants would be worse, or maybe by sharks. "Oh, God," I prayed, standing to my feet, "spare me from such a fate." Thinking about death did not make me feel any more alive, and I continued walking along the shore.

Iona is no stranger to death. Throughout the centuries, Viking Norsemen have raided and gutted its abbey, slaying hundreds of monks and priests. In 806, they slaughtered sixty-eight monks on the beach near the jetty. To this day, it bears the name Martyr's Bay. But others were buried on Iona, too. A small graveyard near Saint Oran's Chapel contains the tombs of sixty kings, forty-eight of them Scottish, eight Norwegian and four Irish. Even Shakespeare's legendary Duncan and his murderer, Macbeth, rest in this graveyard.

The day was passing, the wind was picking up, and I was getting hungry. People are often shocked at the raw power of Iona's wind. The gusts are like invisible walls sweeping the island of pilgrims. At times, the gale-force winds can blow so strongly that it is possible actually to lean hard against them. While I wouldn't suggest trying this on the edge of a cliff, I do think it is an excellent analogy of faith—a faith that supports our body weight when leaning against the invisible.

After trudging around the northwestern part of the island like a headless goose in a hailstorm, I decided to retrace my steps and begin my journey from the safety of square one.

"You look lost," a woman said, appearing behind me.

No words had ever been truer. "I'm trying to get to Saint Columba's Bay," I replied. "Am I close?"

She laughed. Her hair was matted and grey and I assumed the wild wind of Iona was responsible. "Oh, you are really lost," she said. "Columba's Bay is a long way from here."

"How long?"

She thought for a second. "Let's just say it's at the other end of the island."

Great. That wasn't at all what I wanted to hear.

"Give me your map," she said, "and I'll show you the way."

I didn't have a map. "This is such a small island; I didn't think to bring one."

Her smile morphed into a stare. "No map? I have lived on this island for twenty years," she said. "Do you have any idea how many tourists have died here?"

I was hungry, but I wasn't about to swallow that bologna.

"The island of Iona is a natural phenomenon," she explained. "Geologists claim that the rocks and minerals in the soil come from the deepest parts of the earth. Several people have died from falling off the rocks, but most were swallowed by the mud pits."

I couldn't hold back the chuckle. "The mud pits?"

"Why yes, of course," she said. "Their bodies turn up sooner or later."

I sensed a trace of humor in her voice, but I also sensed some seriousness.

"Thanks," I said, "but if I want to make it to Columba's Bay, I better get going." She pointed to the trail. "Just be sure to keep the water to your right, and since you're traveling alone, stay on the path."

Like I needed convincing. I thanked her and followed the ocean until it led me to the split in the trail where I had decided to go right instead of left. A slight drizzle almost convinced me to call it a day and conclude my pilgrimage with an early adventure to our bed-and-breakfast.

Had I been a tourist and not a pilgrim, I would have taken that path. But my mind was resolute, and for me there was no turning back. I was a man on a mission, and my mission was to make it to Saint Columba's Bay no matter what the cost.

I followed the trail for a good distance, but soon it blurred into the landscape and I could not discern its borders. *How do I stay on a trail that disappears?* I wondered. Having played the piano for my whole life, the clarinet for seven years in a concert band and the saxophone for three years in a jazz band (not to mention the kazoo on special occasions), I have learned that improvisation can often save a song no matter how unforgivable the notes. And so I improvised. The main principle to improvisation is to keep the melody moving. You might not hit all the right notes or even the right rhythms, but keep the music flowing and you're bound to end up somewhere.

I ended up somewhere, all right—the middle of an ugly Iona mud pit. No joke. Somewhere between Spouting Cave and Loch Staoineig, I plunged into a pit of mud that was sicker and thicker than anything I knew existed. Perhaps it wasn't mud at all. It was too dense to be mud, too pulling, too jeering, too antagonizing. Whatever it was, I was sinking fast, and the only thing on my mind was Oran, buried alive on this island.

The first step was the worst, and I sank two feet into the filth. Since I was wearing jeans, it was difficult to maneuver my leg since the mud had leeched itself to the heavy denim. Thinking that I had reached the bottom, I took another step into the gooey blackness. Just up ahead I could see the outline of the path, and if I could just plough my way through this pit, I knew I had a chance of reaching it.

I sank down to my thighs. With slurping, sucking noises, the cold mud welcomed me into its marshy home. Strange things pressed against my legs—dead things—plants, roots and perhaps the body parts of those who had been too foolish to bring a map on their adventure. The woman had warned me about this danger, and though I knew the whole ordeal would make for some good giggles in the future (if I survived), at the time I was certainly not giggling. Panicked, I took another step and sank to my waist. "Oh God, don't let me die on this island," I prayed. "Why do I always get stuck in these situations?" It was too far to go back and too cold to stay where I was, and as I considered taking one last step toward the other side, I stopped to analyze the environment.

Here I was, sinking into a slough of despond. In *Pilgrim's Progress*, at least Christian had a friend named Help to save him from his sinking situation. I looked around. There was no help, no friend, not even an angel to pull me from the pit. I was a pilgrim who was making very little progress. Trying to keep my backpack out of the mud, I removed the straps from my shoulders and clutched it to my chest. My camera was inside, but if I had to choose between my camera and my life, I would have happily discarded the camera. I was sinking fast into the earth's Lost and Found, and if God didn't reach down to claim me, it wouldn't be long before the devil reached up to grab me.

Decision time. Did I turn back and run the risk of falling into another pit, or did I lunge forward in the hope that the ground beneath would rise in elevation? The path was clearly in my sight and I prayed with all my might. "All right, God. As silly as this is, I am seriously stuck in a mud pit. You've brought me this far on the journey, now please bring me just a little further, a few sticky feet, so I can pull myself out of this man-eating mire!" Closing my eyes, I made my decision. By the grace and goodness of God Almighty, I mustered my momentum and lunged.

Ground. Another step. Higher ground. Another step. Mudless ground. Another step. Grassy ground! I climbed, pulled and ploughed my way from the pit. Iona's nasty mud poured from my pockets and down the inside of my jeans. My socks were caked in it, my legs were cold from it and even my underwear was smeared with smelly sludge. But I didn't care. I was free! I was breathing! I was happy! "Sorry, Oran," I said, running to the path ahead. "Not this time."

Oh, how I was ready for the brilliant blues, tranquil turquoises and unbelievable aquas awaiting me at Columba's Bay. It was better than the Promised Land. I threw off my shoes, pulled off my socks and washed my hands in the splashing waves. I dipped my head in the water, freeing my curly brown hair from the dried Iona mud. The dirt that had crusted to my legs came loose. And as I sat down on a rock to rinse the brown from my jeans and eat my lunch, I noticed something sparkling on the ground. Bending down, I grabbed a handful of dolphin-green gems. They were just as beautiful as I had imagined. Putting one in my pocket, I prayed over the others and threw them into the sea. They represented several sins in my life that needed to be thrown away (carelessness, particularly), and while they didn't go extremely far, they went far enough to be forgotten.

I suppose those pebbles will return to the shore by the pushing and pulling of tides. An ocean that is constantly contaminated with sinful pebbles must purge itself from time to time. But I imagine that there are too many sins to keep many pebbles from staying too long on the shore. I know mine will go back to the water, one way or another. Who knows, perhaps you will be the one to return them to the waves.

Near the end of his life, Columba was often seen roaming the lonely rocks around Port Ban. At the age of seventy-seven, he is said to have been visited by an angel and told of his upcoming death. Even on his deathbed, his love for calligraphy and Celtic illumination drove him to copy one last psalm before he died: "The lions may grow weak and hungry, / but those who seek the LORD lack no good thing" (Psalm 34:10).

Indeed, Columba lacked no good thing. He helped save many more people than he killed on the Irish battlefield, and without doubt he became one of the greatest Christian fathers in the Celtic world. Magnificent miracles were accomplished through him, even the alleged taming of the Loch Ness monster (which is the first historically documented account of the creature). He founded more than a hundred churches throughout Scotland and England and produced some of the most magnificent copies of the Scriptures ever created. In fact, by the time Pope Gregory the Great saw English slaves wandering the streets of Rome and sent Augustine to convert the Angles, Columba had already become a legend. People far and wide came to Iona to receive his blessing and religious training.

To this day, the island of Iona remains a place of oasis and mystery for the thousands of pilgrims who flock by bus and boat to see its beauty. For such a thin place, it is thick with spiritual blessing. Religious services are held at the abbey in the mornings and evenings, and occasionally ethical and spiritual workshops are offered. While I would highly recommend a walking tour of the island, I ask that you buy a decent map, travel in twos or threes, and if you happen to run into a gray-haired woman at the north end of the island, please tell her that the mud swamps didn't swallow me.

THE CELTIC WAY

Celtic Christianity has become popular in recent years because of its earthiness. In many ways it brings us back into a simple understanding of God and his divine revelation. Celtic Christianity is no clearer expressed than on the animal-filled, pigment-plastered, highly decorated pages of the illuminated Gospels.

Produced by early Celtic scribes like Saint Columba, the outward appearance of the Gospels reflects the Celts' inner appreciation of its truth. So grateful were they that God had communicated with humanity in the form of writing that they tangibly incarnated the preciousness of the Scriptures by copying them with artistic expression. Silver, gold and gems adorned their work. Complex spirals, geometric shapes, woven patterns and meticulous golden knotwork lavished the pages. Months were spent embellishing the words and letters of the Gospels with creative interweavings, decorations and interlinear Celtic drawings. Theirs was a God of art, color and beauty—a God who created the world not in black and white but with the entire spectrum of the rainbow. Theirs was a Christianity on canvas.

Not long after our pilgrimage to Iona, my father and I visited the museum at Trinity College in Dublin, Ireland, that displays the Book of Kells. Walls of information and impressive pictures educate the pilgrim about the process of Celtic illumination. The exhibit explains the pigments, quills and other resources the scribes incorporated into their skill. Since Celtic Christians had no Kinko's to copy their manuscripts, each individual book is unique and filled with personality and character.

The Book of Kells was written about five hundred years after Christ and has often been attributed to the pen of Saint Columba, though the exhibit offers other theories about its origin. In the last room of the exhibit, the pilgrim at last has the opportunity to view the Book of Kells itself. Its pages are turned daily and are most impressive to examine. Time and wear have tainted the vellum, but most of the words and letters retain their vivid color and attractiveness.

Artwork was geared not only for personal enjoyment but also for missionary endeavors. Concerning icons and images, Pope Gregory the Great said that they were "a living reading of the Lord's story for those who cannot read."[2] When Saint Augustine first came to England in 597, he came bearing a silver cross and a picture of Jesus that was painted on a panel. After tearing myself away from the fascinating exhibit, I gained a deeper appreciation not only for the Celts who labored over the embellishing of the Bible but also for the God who, with great patience and determination, produced it throughout the ages.

Recently there has been an interest in and revival of Celtic illumination. Saint John's Abbey in Collegeville, Minnesota, is producing an edition of the Bible in the ancient methods of Celtic illumination. Fully equipped with artwork from hand-ground pigment, the first portion of the Saint John's Bible debuted at the Minneapolis Institute of Art in 2005.

After the invention of the Gutenberg printing press in the 1400s, the duplicating of books became quick and convenient, and the Scriptures were widely circulated throughout the world. Despite this great success, perhaps we have lost something sacred in the process. In the mass production of books, perhaps we have lost the preciousness and uniqueness of the Holy Scriptures.

Celtic manuscripts challenge us to be less haphazard with our Bibles. They teach us to become a people immersed in the Word of God—attached to its ink, plastered to its pages and bound to its binding. Sooner or later, when the world looks at Christians, it will not see the messy sketchings of a caricature; rather, it will see the Word of God expressed through the attractive and artistic pages of a Book of Kells.

Art has always intrigued me. A picture is worth a thousand words, and I have always found it easier to communicate God's truths on canvas than paper. When God created the cosmos, he could have made the world in black and white. He could have drawn lines for trees and circles for stars. He could have emptied the ocean of water and filled it with concrete. The whole world could have been an ashtray, but instead, God made it a rainbow. He took his providential palette and smeared beauty across our globe. He gave us sunsets and shooting stars, waterfalls, monkey grass and dandelions. He water-colored the world with greens, blues, reds and yellows, and he gave us eyes to appreciate them. So when I paint, I participate in this divine activity and re-create what God has already created.

God preserved and accomplished his holy will through artistic endeavors. Preparing to throw his canvas in the water, God told Noah to build a wooden ark that would preserve humanity from total annihilation. He also commanded Moses to make a wooden ark, cover it with gold and place it in the temple. Jesus came into this world via a wooden manger. In his youth he worked with wood, no doubt helping in his father's business. How ironic that the hands of a carpenter would be nailed to a tree. Even today God reveals himself and communicates his truths though wood—pages of the Holy Scriptures. The Celts understood the importance of their Bibles, and they can teach us much about how to read, love and absorb the message of ours.

YOUNGER EVANGELICALS

There is a strange movement sweeping our nation—perhaps you have noticed it. It is a countercultural movement of younger evangelicals who seek to rediscover the biblical, theological and historical heritage of the Christian faith. Disillusioned with shallow, soulless religion, they embrace the non-negotiable elements of the Christian faith: the canon of Scripture, the doctrines of the Bible, the observance of baptism and communion, the preaching of God's Word, the trinitarian and christological dogmas reflected in the early church councils, and the spiritual disciplines derived from the Bible and practiced throughout the history of the church. In his book *The Younger Evangelicals*, Robert Webber explains how these Christians are traveling back to the root system of the Christian faith to claim a deeper and more traditional theology:

> They believe in the God revealed in the great events of creation, incarnation, and re-creation, interpreted first by the prophets and apostles in Scripture, protected in creeds, and handed down to us in the wor-

ship of the church. This is the growing vision of the younger evangelical, a vision that stands within the historic confession of faith.[3]

As a young evangelical, I sense a growing thirst in this country for authentic Christianity. Confused by the modern church and its suffering identity, Christians of the new generation express their desire to reclaim a fresh faith that is holistic and reminiscent of the early apostolic era. In a Celtic sense, young evangelicals appreciate the beauty of God's creation and desire to integrate their Christianity into every aspect of their lives. Insisting on the supreme integrity of the Scriptures, they declare without apology or hesitation that only the historical Jesus who died on a splintery cross for a world of hopeless sinners can satisfy the deepest hungers of the heart. They are pilgrims reclaiming a purpose for their journey.

In the infinity of night skies, in the free flashing of lightning, in whirling elemental winds, you are God. In the impenetrable mists of dark clouds, in the wild gusts of lashing rain, in the ageless rocks of the sea, you are God and I bless you. You are in all things and contained by no thing. You are the Life of all life and beyond every name. You are God and in the eternal mystery I praise you.

CELTIC BENEDICTION

SAINTS, SWORDS AND SAMURAI

Called into Combat

I took the road less traveled by, and that has made all the difference.

ROBERT FROST

Nagasaki, Japan, February 5, 1597

They were forced to take a pilgrimage. It was not a luxurious trip through the Japanese mountains, nor a peaceful stroll through the Japanese pastures. It was a thirty-day death march from Kyoto to Nagasaki. It would be the last journey of their lives, but for the twenty-six Christians walking barefoot through the snow, it was a joyous occasion: they had been considered worthy to suffer for their faith, and heaven was only heartbeats away.

Christianity came to Japan in 1549 when Francis Xavier and two other Jesuits landed on its soil. Fifty years after their arrival, Franciscans from Spain and Jesuits from Portugal were allowed to spread the gospel until 1587, when the Japanese authorities deemed Christianity a threat to their culture. Over the next 260 years, over a million Christians were executed for their faith.

When they arrived at Nishizaka, the lowest hill in Nagasaki, twenty-six crosses awaited them. They were divided into three groups, and each prisoner wanted to know which cross was his. "Is this mine?" Father Ganzalo asked, kneeling before his cross. Peter Baustista stretched out his hands: "Nail them in, brother," he said, disappointed that only ropes and rings were offered. Father Martin exclaimed, "Blessed be the Lord God of Israel, for he has visited and redeemed his people."

Some sang praises, others said creeds. Some whispered Bible verses they had learned as children; others were children, like Anthony, only thirteen years old. John was a little older—nineteen—and he had just become a priest. Twelve-year-old Louis Ibaraki was hanging beside John, his soprano voice screaming, "Paradise! Paradise!" They were all deep in prayer, thanking God for his blessings on them and praying for those who were watching the executions.

Terazawa Hazaburo, the executioner, could watch no more. The crowds were being evangelized by the suffering prisoners, and many were coming to know Jesus. Once the Christians had been tied to the crosses, they were simultaneously lifted and placed in the ground. Paul Miki began to preach, arms outstretched. "I have committed no crime," he said to the crowd of people, "and the only reason why I am put to death is that I have been teaching the doctrine of our Lord Jesus Christ. I am happy to die for such a cause and see my death as the greatest blessing from the Lord. At this critical time, when you can rest assured that I will not try to deceive you, I want to stress and make it unmistakably clear that man can find no salvation other than the Christian way."[1] The guards inched near his cross, taking in his every word.

Terazawa Hazaburo was a seasoned soldier of war. Having grown up respecting the code of the samurai, he knew the importance of dying a good death. The code says:

> The foremost concern of a warrior, no matter what his rank, is how he will behave at the moment of his death. No matter how eloquent and intelligent you may normally seem to be, if you lose composure on the brink of death and die in an unseemly manner, your previous good conduct will all be in vain, and you will be looked down upon by serious people. This is a very disgraceful thing.[2]

Terazawa had seen many people die, but never had he witnessed such honor and courage than by the Christians he had just killed. Not even the death of a samurai could compare to the death of a saint; theirs was a faith unlike any he had ever known, a belief system worth bleeding for, a God worth dying for. Tears streamed down his cheeks as Terazawa turned and walked away.

Nagasaki, Japan, 1995

According to an ancient legend, the islands of Japan were formed when the tears of the gods mingled with the waters of the earth. I felt like crying, too, as I looked down at the on-flight meal sitting on my tray. Later I would develop a strong affinity for Japanese food, but this was my first experience, and though the entrée looked dead enough, I didn't have the guts to poke it and find out.

After an exhausting twenty-three hours of travel from Birmingham, Alabama, to Seoul, South Korea, via a layover in Portland, Oregon, my father and I arrived in Asia more jet-lagged than we'd ever been. We stayed several days with our missionary friends Dr. and Mrs. Charles D. Sands and then traveled to Taejon where my father lectured at the Korea Baptist Theological Seminary. After taking a six-hour excursion to a Buddhist monastery in the Korean mountains, we traveled to Suwon, where our friend and former president of the Baptist World Alliance, Billy Kim, served as pastor of Suwon Central Baptist Church.

It was Sunday morning. I stood before a sea of swarming black hair, ebbing and flowing and mesmerizing me as I raised the microphone to my mouth. Never had I seen such a sight. Almost three thousand young Korean Christians watched me. They must have noticed my shaking legs and sweaty brow, but I was eager to share my testimony with them.

Korea claims a history that is roughly five thousand years old. Its story contains foreign invaders, power-hungry monarchs and ruthless wars. Amazingly enough, South Korea has become a beacon of light to Asia, spreading the gospel with great boldness to its neighbors. With the exception of the Philippines, South Korea has the highest percentage of Christians in East and Southeast Asia, some 35 percent of the population.

Pilgrims flock to South Korea to pray. It has long been the practice for Korean Christians to assemble at five o'clock in the morning, seven days a week, for hours of communication with God. More than one million Koreans do this every year, and when I attended one of their prayer meetings, I was shocked. Hundreds of Christians imploring God, pursuing and wrestling with him to listen. Their vigorous enthusiasm for the discipline caught me off guard, and while I was still wiping the sleep from my eyes, the Koreans beside me were energetically engaging God, pulling his holy presence down into the green hills of their country.

I asked myself, *What is prayer, anyway?* Is it a grocery list of my wants and needs? Is it a credit card I use to purchase earthly possessions? Perhaps prayer is a mirror, reflecting the true ambitions of my heart. Perhaps it is a window, revealing the hidden face of God.

Libraries of books have been written about prayer. For Francois Fénelon, prayer is "simply another name for the love of God."[3] For Oswald Chambers, prayer is "not what it costs us, but what it cost God to enable us to pray."[4] For Henri Nouwen, prayer is "standing in the presence of God with the mind in the heart."[5] For Dudley Hall it is "incense going up before the altar of God."[6] Jesus instructs us to pray to our Father who is unseen (Matthew 6:6). Paul commands us to pray without ceasing (1 Thessalonians 5:17). Peter reminds us that God's ears listen to our prayers (1 Peter 3:12).

Being in a Korean prayer meeting changed any of my former definitions of prayer. For me, prayer became less of a sentence and more of a sound—sighs and cries from the deepest parts of the soul. Prayer is that noise a bottle of soda makes when the cap is twisted off—*psssss*. After life has shaken us up and pressurized us with the pain and problems of everyday events, the Holy Spirit comes and "intercedes for us with groans that words cannot express" (Romans 8:26), and our prayers spew into the presence of God. Indeed, we are carbonated Christians praying to a thirsty God.

From Taejon we traveled back to Seoul to catch a plane to Fukuoka, Japan. When I was a young boy, my grandfather often told me stories about

Japan. When he was only fifteen, he lied and said he was eighteen in order to enlist as a merchant marine during World War II. In those days, the land troops required supply ships to carry ammunition, food and machinery to the front lines. It was a dangerous job and many supply ships were sunk by the Japanese resistance. My grandfather served on one of these ships, and I remember his stories as if they were my own—the smell of oil beneath the deck, the splash of saltwater against the ship, the sound of gunfire from the shore.

I couldn't wait to set my feet on Japanese soil and see this part of the world for myself. Greeting us at the Fukuoka airport was our missionary friend Gary Barkley. We stayed with him and his family for several days, then traveled by train to Nagasaki, where we entered the World War II museum.

On the morning of August 9, 1945, an American B-29 flown by Major Charles W. Sweeney carried the second atomic bomb, "Fat Man," to the city of Kokura. Because of cloud interference, he proceeded to fly to his next target, Nagasaki. Containing approximately 6.4 kilograms of plutonium-239, the atomic bomb exploded over Nagasaki at an altitude of 1,540 feet. In one split second, seventy-five thousand people were killed and Nagasaki's population dropped from 422,000 to 383,000. As a prelude to the main exhibits, a museum clock is stopped at 11:02 a.m., the exact minute of the explosion. Melted human bodies are displayed behind glass exhibits—bones and bottles fused together from the heat of the explosion. Ninety-five percent of the casualties were civilians, and those who did survive the blast, called *hibakusha* (bomb-affected people), still suffer from radiation exposure today. If C. S. Lewis was right and "God whispers to us in our pleasures, speaks in our conscience, but shouts in our pain,"[7] God must have become hoarse in this part of the world over the last five hundred years.

After leaving the museum and visiting the Nishizaka hill in Nagasaki where the twenty-six martyrs were killed, I developed an admiration for those who were willing to sacrifice their lives for the advancement of the kingdom of God. A bronze wall marks the spot of the martyrs' executions. Their statues are lined up in the order of their crucifixions. As we walked by the bronze figures, my eye drifted to one of the younger martyrs, a boy about my age. He was barely twelve years old but had the courage of a seasoned saint. I wanted that courage. I wanted that kind of commitment to Christ. Christianity cost him everything, and he was obedient to the Lord's instruction even to the point of death.

From Nagasaki we traveled to Hiroshima to see where the first atomic bomb, "Little Boy," exploded. Like the museum in Nagasaki, it churns a pilgrim's stomach to walk through this museum's halls. The gruesome reality of war pervaded much of our pilgrimage to southern Japan, but it forced me to confront my own understanding of spiritual warfare and my responsibility as a soldier of Christ.

Christians are called into combat. Paul writes, "For our struggle is not against flesh and blood, but against the rulers, against the authorities, against the powers of this dark world and against the spiritual forces of evil in the heavenly realms" (Ephesians 6:12-13). I'll never forget the story of Martin of Tours, after whom the great reformer Martin Luther was named. One day during the Middle Ages, Saint Martin was praying in his room and an angel of light appeared. Thinking it was Jesus himself, Saint Martin fell to his knees in worship. But while he was worshiping on his knees, Martin glanced up. Something about this creature seemed strange. Something was wrong. Something was missing. Rising to his feet, Saint Martin pointed to the creature's hands and asked, "Where are the nail prints? Show me the nail prints!" Instantly, the creature vanished into the darkness, never to return.

Demons won't ignore us if we threaten their kingdom. The brighter we shine, the easier they see us. They may trick us, tempt us and whisper sweet nothings of evil in our ears, but if we fight beneath the flag of Jesus Christ, God has us in his hand. And so fixed are we within those fingers that not a hand from the pit of hell can reach up and pull us into the flames.

Spiritual combat demands that we train like a soldier, study like a scholar, meditate like a monk and pray like a puritan. In doing so we can overcome our tendency to slip into complacency, and day after day we will become a greater threat to the kingdom of Satan.

According to the legend of Saint George, a local village was being terror-
ized by a hideous dragon. Every day the villagers appeased the beast by sac-
rificing two sheep for its consumption. When the dragon tired of sheep it
demanded humans, but no one in the town wanted to be the first to be
eaten. Lots were cast, and the lot fell on the king's only daughter. Great
mourning filled the day that the king's daughter dressed herself as a bride
and approached the hungry monster. Saint George, however, arrived on the
scene with spear in hand. He was, after all, a knight in pursuit of a princess.
With a fast flick of the wrist, he threw his lance at the neck of the creature
and slayed it with his sword. The girl was saved, the day was won, and the
village no longer had a dragon to fear.

Now, I'm no knight in shining armor and no one's ever called me "Saint
George," but I do believe we all have our dragons to slay. Some of us have
dragons of doubt, pride and fear. Others have dragons of lust, envy and
greed. They follow us by day and stalk us by night. Sometimes we can ignore
them, but if we are to defeat them, we first must face them. With the power
of God's help, Christians are called to take our lances and slay the sinful habits where they lie.

In John Bunyan's *Pilgrim's Progress,* Christian fought a scaly dragon
named Apollyon. Here's my recap of the battle:

"Where do you think you're going?" the creature growled.

Christian replied, "I'm going to the Celestial City, and I serve the King of
Kings."

The fiend flashed with fury. "I hate the king and I hate his people. Prepare
yourself for death!"

Apollyon hurled a flaming arrow at Christian's head, which would have
killed him were it not for Christian's shield of faith with which he deflected
the attack.

"Be careful, Apollyon," Christian shouted. "You're standing on the king's
highway and you're in my way!"

The creature recoiled and threw himself at the pilgrim. Christian fell
backwards—thrashing, slashing and bashing against the beast. Apollyon's fi-

ery breath browned Christian's breastplate of righteousness. Teeth and claws tore at his armor. For half a day they dueled until Christian grew tired and could no longer defend himself against the demon's onslaught.

"I have you now!" Apollyon shouted, knocking Christian's sword from his hand.

The creature stood on its hind legs, about to deliver the final blow. Apollyon had defeated millions of souls this way. Bruised, beaten and bloodied, Christian began to pray. He prayed with every ounce of strength he could muster, and as he lay on his back, defenseless and exposed, his fingers found a familiar object—the sword of the Spirit.

"Do not gloat over me, my enemy!" Christian shouted. "Though I have fallen, I will rise!" Suddenly, Christian thrust his sword into the warm belly of the beast, sending Apollyon squealing into the sky. Christian had defeated his dragon and he continued on his way, carrying his sword of the Spirit closely to his side.

The samurai sword is a marvelous work of art. Unlike the swords used by medieval knights in Europe or barbaric Scandinavian Vikings, the samurai sword sometimes took up to a year to forge. The heated metal was welded and cooled thousands of times before it was ready for combat. By the time it reached the warrior's hand, most of the impurities were removed and its blade could cut through even the thickest of earthly elements.

The Christian, too, has a sword. The author of Hebrews reminds us that "the word of God is living and active. Sharper than any double-edged sword, it penetrates even to dividing soul and spirit, joints and marrow" (Hebrews 4:12). The samurai took a whole year to weld a sword, but God took thousands of years to bring his sacred sword into being. Through the prophets and apostles, he hammered his Holy Word to completion, and it remains a weapon without impurity, slicing through sinews and penetrating into the deepest parts of the soul. When Jesus went into the wilderness to be tempted by the devil, the sword of the Spirit was his weapon of choice, and he thwarted his dragon's attack with the wounding words, "It is written."

From Hiroshima, we traveled to the former capital of Japan, Kyoto, and stayed with our friends John and Nancy Norton. After touring ancient Japanese gardens and tea houses, we concluded our pilgrimage by jumping on the bullet train to Tokyo before flying back to America.

Our trip to Asia opened my eyes to many things. The stark contrast between the spiritual hunger of South Korea and the spiritual poverty of Japan shocked me. The gospel that thrives in Korea has barely influenced Japan, and though missionaries are engaging the Japanese culture more aggressively than ever before, the contrast between these two countries is startling. The moving example of the Nagasaki martyrs and their unapologetic dedication to the gospel inspired me and reminded me that I was not too young to give my life to Christ. As a Christian I am called into combat, and if my life is lost on the battlefield, it will be considered a blessing, a duty and an honor.

WISDOM FROM THE DOJO

They lunged at her from all directions, six grown men against one middle-aged woman. She didn't have a prayer's hope of survival. The opponents pulled no punches and kept no kicks. Their goal was simple, their mission easy. And like lightning striking a tree, they attempted to throw the woman to the mat.

But suddenly, the tree began to sway. In a whirlwind of spinning grey hair, she sprung into action—passive action. When someone struck her, she embraced the strike and redirected its momentum. When someone shoved her, she absorbed the movement and swirled the attack to her advantage. No one could touch her; she was like water trickling over the stones of a riverbed. She borrowed their balance and returned it to them with grace, agility and accuracy. She did not think or plan but only reacted to the changing environment, and her reactions sent her opponents spinning across the room. At the end of it all, a seemingly fragile, middle-aged woman had single-handedly transformed six strong men into clumsy little boys.

It's called aikido. Upon seeing this demonstration in a dojo, I dedicated several years of my life to learning it. I have always believed that God wants

Christians to push the gospel beyond the walls of the church. To this end, and because of my incurable curiosity for every kind of art, I decided to take the gospel into the heart of the dojo (training area). The first year or so was difficult—learning to absorb punches, execute rolls and fight with Okinawan weapons like swords, staffs and knives. But eventually, I earned the respect of those around me, shared the gospel with several friends and advanced in my aikido training.

Unlike karate and *jeet kune do* (Bruce Lee's mixture of *wing chun*, boxing and fencing), I have found aikido (the way of harmony) the most educational—if I see you getting beat up, I'll certainly come to your aid. Drawing from techniques of the ancient samurai, Morihei Ueshiba created the art of aikido in the 1920s.

In Japanese, the word *samurai* means "servant." Contrary to modern stereotypes, most samurai were devout artists, poets, potters, musicians and athletes. They lived in peace and while they were sufficiently trained for combat, they resorted to war with grave hesitation. Morihei Ueshiba incorporated this respect for life and peace into his art form. The goal of aikido is not to hurt or harm the opponent, but rather to maintain peace using leverage, balance and joint manipulations. Peace is the ultimate goal, and after the atomic bomb exploded over Hiroshima to end World War II, Morihei optimistically said of his country, "Instead of foolishly waging war, hereafter we will wage peace, the true purpose of Aikido. We will train to prevent war, to abolish nuclear weapons, to protect the environment, and to serve society."[8] Truly Morihei Ueshiba embodied the essence of samurai servanthood, and his discipline is practiced all across the globe.

Aikido has much to teach the pilgrim. Since the path curves and changes without warning, one must practice fluidity, flexibility and agility to stay on it. Changing environments demand elasticity.

"Houston, we have a problem." These words are forever ingrained in our American consciousness. The pilgrims aboard Apollo 13 never saw it coming. They were on a mission to the moon, but at two hundred thousand miles from earth, in the middle of a quiet cosmos, an oxygen tank exploded.

Their pilgrimage to the moon became a struggle for survival. Their air was low, their options depleted, and the best engineers on earth were wracking their brains for solutions. One last idea came to the floor. Instead of landing on the moon like the original plan called for, the astronauts needed to borrow its energy and circle around it, using the moon's gravitational field to thrust their vessel back to earth. Instead of opposing the problem, they harmonized with it. The original blueprints for the journey were modified, and although hope seemed light years in the distance, the revised plan of action brought them safely home.

The pilgrim journey is packed with problems, but instead of resisting the hardships—jet lag, motion sickness, missed flights, lost luggage, bad food—it's best to blend with them and learn from them. Bruce Lee, a Chinese martial artist, informs us about the art of adaptability:

> Water is so fine that it is impossible to grasp a handful of it; strike it, yet it does not suffer hurt; stab it, and it is not wounded; sever it, and yet it is not divided. It has no shape but molds itself to the receptacle that contains it. . . . Now you put water into a cup, it becomes the cup. You pour water into a bottle, it becomes a bottle. You put water into a teapot, it becomes a teapot. Now water can flow or creep or drip—or crash! Be water, my friend.[9]

Each inconvenience and disturbance teaches us something sacred about ourselves, our faith and the God who himself was familiar with suffering. Like water rising to find its level, Christians flow across desert, stone and ocean until, at last, we reach our Father who is in heaven.

The Lord my Shepherd,
there is nothing I shall want,
grazing in His fields.

To quiet waters
He leads me; and as I rest
He revives my soul.

By paths of virtue
He, for the sake of His name,
lovingly leads me.

Even in darkness
no evil will befall me,
no harm do I fear.

Your rod and your staff
will be of comfort to me,
signs of Your nearness.

In sight of my foes
You set me at Your table,
offer me choice foods.

You anoint my head
with the richness of Your oils.
My cup brims over.

Oh, how much goodness!
You pursue me with kindness
each day of my life.

Thus shall it be, Lord:
my home, the house of Yahweh
as long as I live!

Father Richard Gwyn, Psalm 23 in haiku

SACRED SONGS

Chanting from the Heart

After silence, that which comes nearest to expressing the inexpressible is music.

ALDOUS HUXLEY

Taizé, France, October 5, 1986

Pope John Paul II surveyed the scene. Thousands of pilgrims had come to Taizé for prayer, spiritual guidance and singing. After praying with the crowd on the side of the hill, the pope met with the monks of Taizé to encourage them and commend their spiritual vigor:

> Each of you came here to live in the mercy of God and the community of his brothers. In consecrating your whole being to Christ for love of him, you have found both of these. . . . By desiring to be yourselves a "parable of community," you will help all whom you meet to be faithful to their denominational ties, the fruit of their education and their choice in conscience, but also to enter more and more deeply into the mystery of communion that the Church is in God's plan.[1]

The founder of Taizé, Brother Roger Schutz, was born in Switzerland on May 12, 1915. At the age of twenty-five, God called him to begin a community where Christians of various denominations could live with one another. His lifelong battle with tuberculosis sensitized him to the sufferings of others, and he sought to create an environment of peace and love in the midst of war and pain.

In the small village of Taizé, a few miles from the demarcation line that split France in half during World War II, Roger established a community of simplicity and hospitality that welcomed refugees of war. Seeking to live out the essential truths of the Christian faith, Roger and his sister, Genevieve, harbored Jews who were seeking shelter from the horrors of the German concentration camps. Food and water were in short supply, but they persisted in offering relief to those whose lives were endangered.

In the autumn of 1942, the hospitality of Taizé was revealed to the authorities and Roger was forced to leave. In 1944, however, he returned with several monks to develop a monastic way of life. Chants and prayers were written for the Taizé community, and they invented a monastic rule. Committing themselves to celibacy and sharing, the monks of Taizé grew in number and popularity. Pilgrims throughout France and Europe sought to worship with the brothers, and Taizé once again opened its doors for shelter and hospitality.

To this day, more than five thousand young people from more than seventy-five countries visit the community of Taizé annually to participate in singing, worship and Bible studies during the summer months. In an age of religious terrorism and division, people of all faiths flock to Taizé for a week of spiritual renewal and revival.

Church leaders also frequent the community. Taizé has housed three archbishops of Canterbury, fourteen Lutheran bishops of Sweden and thousands of pastors from across the world. Grateful that Taizé works toward Christian unity, Pope John Paul II concluded his speech with these words:

> You know how much I personally consider ecumenism a necessity incumbent upon me, a pastoral priority in my ministry for which I count on your prayer. . . . Dear Brothers, I thank you for having invited me and thus having given me the opportunity to return to Taizé. May the Lord bless you and keep you in his peace and his love![2]

Taizé, France, 1999

We filed into the dark sanctuary—silent, contemplative and hungry. We were silent because it was required, contemplative because it was silent and hungry because our previous meals had been somewhat less than filling. After three days of watery soup, questionable meat and crunchy bread, I felt like a medieval monk, surviving on prayer and poverty. Would I survive another day in this monastic camp? Could I last a little longer in this environment? I didn't know. But I suppose pilgrimage and gluttony have never been good friends, and we certainly did not come to Taizé to dine.

We came to worship.

Every year, tens of thousands of Christians, Buddhists, Hindus, God-searchers and other spiritual seekers travel to Taizé to worship, pray and chant. Today Taizé is an international ecumenical community composed of more than one hundred monks from Catholic and various Protestant backgrounds from more than twenty-five nations. Pilgrims who travel to Taizé are invited to join the corporate worship services, which occur three times a day—8:15 a.m., 12:20 p.m. and 8:30 p.m. At first this schedule seemed demanding (especially since I was accustomed to going to church only three times a week), but soon it seeped into the bloodstream.

From Paris we had come to the city of Dijon, where we stayed with our evangelical missionary friends David Bjork and his family. After eating a meal of cheese and snails in a small French chateaux, David Riker, David Bjork, my father and I embarked by car on a pilgrimage to Taizé, two miles north of Cluny.

When we entered the camp, we were educated about its history and purpose and then segregated into two groups: people under thirty and people over thirty. Being the youngest, I was split from my fellow pilgrims and accommodated in a dormitory in a different location in the camp. Most pilgrims bring tents to Taizé because of the large fields suitable for pitching, but personally, I would recommend the dormitories—rustic cabins equipped with blankets, pillows and beds. Since Taizé is a place of rugged spirituality, deep contemplation and monastic austerity, the comfortable luxuries of home should not be expected.

The sanctuary at Taizé is the center of life for the community. It's called the Church of Reconciliation, and its name suggests its purpose. The architecture is modern, simple and intentional. The Church of Reconciliation has no choir. Everyone who attends the Taizé worship is a member of the choir, and together they chant on mats that face the front of the church.

My mat was orange. The lighting was low, but I could see the faces beside me—faces contorted in prayer. Candles flickered here and there, but they did not distract me from the growing silence within. I closed my eyes and prepared my heart to encounter the God who speaks to those who are listening. I was not accustomed to this. There were no bands, drums, yelling or chatter to distract my wandering mind from worshiping my fathomless God. Just silence, inward reflection, spiritual preparation. I had no excuse anymore; God would have to be the focus of my heart.

And then the chanting. It began quietly and did not disrupt the atmosphere. In fact, it reminded me of the reason we had come together—singing together the praises of God. Being a Baptist, chanting did not come easy to me. To be honest, Monty Python had taught me everything I knew about the discipline, and even that wasn't much! What was the purpose of singing Latin words to broken melodies and repetitious tunes?

Brother Roger and the monks of Taizé wrote their own chants. They are simple little songs, easy to sing and catchy to hum. Some are sung in French and German, others in Latin and English. All of them are thoroughly christocentric, biblically based and fundamentally evangelical. Before the worship service, we were all handed Taizé songbooks. The light was low and the chanting had already begun, but I opened to the front page and read the inscription:

> Singing is one of the most important forms of prayer. A few words sung over and over again reinforce the meditative quality of the prayer. They express a basic reality of faith that can quickly be grasped by the intellect, and that gradually penetrates the heart and the whole being. These simple chants also provide a way of praying when one is alone, during the day or at night, or even in the silence of one's heart while one is working.[3]

The mat beneath me was not the pew I was used to, but it forced my back to arch and my lungs to expand. *Bonum est confidere in Domino, bonum sperare in Domino.* Again, we sang the song. "It is good to trust in the Lord our God, trust and hope in the Lord our God."

We repeated again. *Bonum est confidere in Domino, bonum sperare in Domino.* Over and over again. "It is good to trust in the Lord our God, trust and hope in the Lord our God."

Music joined in. *Bonum est confidere in Domino, bonum sperare in Domino.* Breathing became rhythmic. "It is good to trust in the Lord our God, trust and hope in the Lord our God."

Time disappeared. *Bonum est confidere in Domino, bonum sperare in Domino.*

Singing became natural. "It is good to trust in the Lord our God, trust and hope in the Lord our God."

Harmonization. *Bonum est confidere in Domino, bonum sperare in Domino.* Worship.

Fifteen minutes later when the chant ended, I opened my eyes. What on earth had I just experienced? My heart was quiet, my attention upward, and deep within my mind the melody kept moving, reminding me over and over again of how good it is to trust and hope in God. The service was odd and unfamiliar, but I couldn't wait until the next song began. After an hour or so of worship, the service dismissed and we quietly left the sanctuary.

By the end of the week, I was ready to become a monk. Oh, I had it all planned out. For starters, I was going to shave my head and take the vow of celibacy. Wait, never mind. I could never be a monk. But I was certainly hooked on chanting. I anticipated every time we met in the sanctuary, and I lived from one service to the next, lost in the rhythm of worship, immersed in the beauty of simplicity, eager to incorporate the elements of the Taizé experience into my devotional life.

Instead of the microwavable music I was used to—songs finished in forty seconds or less—Taizé introduced me to a new way to worship, a slow-cooker approach. Instead of blurring through hymns at light speed, I understood the importance of slowing down the song to allow its spiritual meat to simmer in the crock pot of my consciousnesses.

After a week at Taizé, I developed a distaste for spiritual fast food—worship that takes no time to prepare and leaves me feeling empty and hollow. God deserves more praise from me than that. The chanting of Taizé freed my songs of praise to fall from my head where I knew them, to my heart where I felt them, to my hands where I could live them. Nothing else mattered. Appointments couldn't antagonize me, schedules couldn't stalk me, and with hundreds of people around me in that dark sanctuary, I worshiped God on my little orange mat.

To this day, I'll be driving in my car, studying for an exam or falling asleep at night, and those sacred songs will pop into my head. In the midnight moments—hospital moments—I hum their harmonies, and suddenly I'll be back on my knees, chanting those simple words of spiritual encouragement. Taizé brought fresh ingredients to my understanding of worship, and those rhythmic melodies continue to remind me of how good it is to trust the Lord. I pray they will follow me all the way to my deathbed.

ON GOD AND LOVE

His name was Sören. Born and bred in Sweden, he didn't know many Americans. After we met the first night in Taizé, I discovered that he was an atheist. It perplexed me that an atheist would travel all the way from Sweden to participate in the worship of this community, but we quickly became friends and stayed up the first night talking about life, God and what it was like to live in a land with a 60-percent income tax.

The next morning Sören hugged me. It was not a normal guy-to-guy locker room hug—I've had plenty of those. No, this was something altogether different, and I took my subsequent morning shower with great speed and determination.

"How's it going, Christian?" Sören asked, stepping into the shower.

God have mercy. "Um, pretty good, thanks," I said, dressing as fast as I could. "So I'll see you in the sanctuary later?" he asked.

I paused. Here I was in the middle of France, worshiping in a community that embraces people of all types, but because of my own prejudices I didn't want to meet Sören in the worship service. Why? This was a marvelous missionary opportunity, but I was reluctant to engage in evangelism, and I was even more reluctant to pursue this friendship any farther.

But then God got hold of me. When Pope John Paul II came to Taizé, he sat down in a wooden chair and told a youth group, "One passes through Taizé as one passes close to a spring of water. The traveler stops, quenches his thirst and continues on his way."[4] God reminded me that nothing happens by accident. Perhaps he had brought me to Taizé not only to learn about the depth of worship and the beauty of chanting but also the importance of being Christ to those around me. Perhaps I was here because Sören was here, so I looked over at him in the shower. "Yeah, I'll see you later in church."

My life is full of moments when God pulls on the reins and redirects my path. King David warns me that I should not be like "the horse or the mule, / which have no understanding / but must be controlled by bit and bridle" (Psalm 32:9), but often I am too busy cantering through the pastures of carnality to notice.

"I don't believe that God exists," Sören said later that night. He was lying in a bunk bed beside mine. The lights were out for the night and talking was not permitted.

"Why?" I whispered.

"Many reasons," he replied. "It was my friend's idea to come to Taizé, but I'm glad I came—there are some really hot guys here." He looked over at me.

I cringed. I wanted to end the conversation right then and there, but something inside me urged the conversation onward. "Sören, why don't you believe in God?"

"Can't see him, touch him, taste him, hear him or smell him." He laughed. "How can I believe in something like that?"

I knew that great answers existed for those kinds of questions—ontological and epistemological answers. There are many arguments that prove the existence of God. From Anselm to Augustine to Aquinas, I was prepared to hit every period of every point of every proof, and it was going to be beautiful. A little C. S. Lewis, some Francis Schaeffer, not to mention a dab of Alvin Plantinga.

But then I reconsidered.

Through the history of Christianity, souls have been saved not through lecture but through love. I thought of D. L. Moody and how he literally loved his congregations into heaven. So I shut the theological file cabinets I was digging through and closed the philosophical books I was reading from, and throwing it all to the wind of the Holy Spirit, I inquired, "So, do you believe in love?"

He paused. He wasn't expecting that kind of question. "Love? Well, yes, I believe in love."

"Even though you can't see it, explain it or scientifically contain it?" I asked.

"I believe in love because I can feel it," he said. "And my feelings are emotional responses to my environment."

"So what if I told you that God wants you to feel him?" I asked. "What if I believe that he wants to create an emotional response within you?"

He grinned and threw a pillow at me.

I threw it back.

"Don't get your hopes up," he said, turning on his side.

Too late. I prayed for Sören's conversion until I fell asleep. Every evening we discussed the probability of the existence of God and the possibility that God, if he indeed existed, could love his creatures into loving him back. At times it was exhausting, but in the end, I knew that if Sören ever came to believe in the God we were chanting about in church, it would be the result of relentless relationships, not relentless arguments.

I haven't heard from Sören since that week in Taizé, but he is often the subject of my thoughts and prayers. If someone had told me that I, a heterosexual Christian, would befriend a homosexual atheist and share intimate thoughts about eternity with him, I would have recoiled. But God knew what he was doing, and although I am straighter than a starched white shirt, he knew that my friendship with Sören would expose the wrinkled areas of sin and self-righteousness that otherwise might have remained untamed, unchanged and unchallenged.

In the Middle Ages, pilgrims returning home were called palmers because they carried palm branches to indicate that they had been on a spiritual journey. As our week at Taizé ended and our journey through Europe continued, we, too, were palmers returning from a sacred journey. But instead of carrying palms in our hands, we chanted songs in our hearts. After five days of rhythmic monastic worship, it was difficult to plunge back into the arduous pace of travel. As the beautiful gardens of Taizé disappeared behind us, I came to understand why Pope John XXIII once said, "Ah, Taizé, that little Springtime!"[5]

On August 16, 2005, a thirty-six-year-old Romanian woman with schizophrenia visited the Taizé community. During the evening worship service in the Church of Reconciliation, she approached Brother Roger and slit his throat with a knife. Twenty-five hundred pilgrims witnessed the incident, and several minutes later the saint who founded the community of Taizé became its first and only martyr. The woman was apprehended by the crowd, arrested and placed in confinement.

Brother Roger centered his entire life on the foundation of gentleness, hospitality and forgiveness. Having spoken personally with him, I am confident that he would have harbored no hatred toward this woman, but rather his words would have reflected Christ's words: Father, forgive her, for she knows not what she did.

AND ALL THAT JAZZ

Pilgrimage is music in motion. The jazzy notes are fluid, spontaneous and unpredictable. The tune is always changing—dipping, rising, filled with happy harmonies and melancholy melodies. There are deep valleys and high hills, low notes and high notes, blue notes and sharp notes. The musician who taps his foot to the tune and the pilgrim who taps his foot to the trail both go into the future blindly, trusting that in the end the song will be sweet to the ear and even sweeter to the step.

When we follow the leader's steps—spinning, swirling, swinging—we stay close to God, mesmerized by his voice, captured by his movement. We don't know where the steps will lead us or how the rhythm will flow; we are too in love to look. Around the floor we go, caught up in the moment, humming, "I need thee every hour, most gracious Lord; no tender voice like thine can peace afford." Suddenly, we realize that our journey is not only taking us to God, but God is going with us on the journey. And he assures us that earth is not our final dance, it is only a dress rehearsal until Christ escorts us into eternity.

Pilgrimage finds its ultimate fulfillment in the worship of God. When David went to the temple, he said, "I rejoiced with those who said to me, 'Let us go to the house of the LORD'" (Psalm 122:1). Worshiping God does not require a pilgrimage, but sacred journeys do open our eyes to the God who is worthy of worship from all living things. From the whistling of the trees to the blowing of the breeze, the earth itself adores its Creator, and pilgrimage enlarges our understanding of him.

According to Zephaniah 3:17, God rejoices over us with singing. He is so proud of his creation, so enthralled with those who rejoice in him, that he celebrates with all the facilities of his being. Music is a divine institution. C. S. Lewis plays on this theme in *The Magician's Nephew* when Aslan sings Narnia into existence. Singing fulfills its original design when we incorporate it into our worship services. We sing because we serve a God who sings, and at the heart of Christian worship is our opportunity to reflect God's creative gifts back onto him.

Humans were made for music. The Israelites, some of the earliest biblical pilgrims, incorporated music into their lives as they journeyed to the Promised Land. When Saul was inflicted by an evil spirit, David played music for him on the lyre and the spirit fled (1 Samuel 16:14-23). Before the Israelites left the Red Sea, the book of Exodus records:

Miriam the prophetess, Aaron's sister, took a tambourine in her hand,

and all the women followed her, with tambourines and dancing. Miriam sang to them:

"Sing to the Lord,
    for he is highly exalted.
The horse and its rider
    he has hurled into the sea."

Then Moses led Israel from the Red Sea and they went into the Desert of Shur. (Exodus 15:20-22)

When David built the temple of God, he incorporated a ministry of music there. "All these men were under the supervision of their fathers for the music of the temple of the Lord, with cymbals, lyres and harps, for the ministry at the house of God" (1 Chronicles 25:6). Music is ingrained throughout the Old Testament and reflects our deepest expressions of praise to God.

The book of Psalms is a collection of Hebrew poetry originally set to music. Psalm 147:7 declares, "Sing to the LORD with thanksgiving; / make music to our God on the harp." Many pilgrims who have obeyed this command have found identification with and comfort in the practice. According to the Talmud, certain psalms should be sung for each day of the week: the first day Psalm 24, the second day Psalm 48, the third day Psalm 82, the fourth day Psalm 94, the fifth day Psalm 81, the sixth day Psalm 93, and on the Sabbath day Psalm 92 (Talmud VII:3). Such regular and rhythmic worship motivates us to become a people who are serious about exalting Christ and developing a deep devotional life.

In the early stages of Christianity, music and worship were fundamental to the Christian's journey through life. Paul encouraged the saints in Ephesus to "speak to one another with psalms, hymns and spiritual songs. Sing and make music in your heart to the Lord" (Ephesians 5:19).

Around A.D. 111, Pliny the Younger, the Roman governor of Bithynia and Pontus, wrote to Emperor Trajan to discuss the outbreak of Christians. He observed their worship service and reported that Christians would assemble on a certain day before dawn and "sing a hymn among themselves to the

Christ."[6] Threatened by Christianity, the Roman Empire began persecuting believers. Ironically, the body of Christ performs most healthily when it's under the most strenuous exercise, and the persecution of the church fueled the spread of Christianity. According to Saint Augustine:

> A hymn is a song containing praise of God. If you praise God, but without song, you do not have a hymn. If you praise anything which does not pertain to the glory of God, even if you sing it, you do not have a hymn. Hence, a hymn contains the three elements: song and praise of God.[7]

From the hot sands of Africa to the isolated shores of Skellig Michael, hymns containing song and praise to God became an important element in the daily Christian liturgy.

At the beginning of the eleventh century, hymns and chants evolved with ornate and impressive complexity. Musical notation allowed melodies to be recorded on paper instead of sung from memory, and chanting developed into an elaborate artform. Cathedrals were constructed with choirs, and pilgrims traveled hundreds of miles to experience not only the grandeur of the architecture but also the splendor of worship.

By the time of the Protestant Reformation in the 1500s, Christian music was a primary religious activity. Martin Luther, an Augustinian monk, was deeply steeped in the tradition of chanting and singing. His words reflect the power of music and its inherent therapeutic significance:

> Next to the Word of God, music deserves the highest praise. She is a mistress and governess of those human emotions . . . which control men or more often overwhelm them. . . . Whether you wish to comfort the sad, to subdue frivolity, to encourage the despairing, to humble the proud, to calm the passionate, or to appease those full of hate . . . what more effective means than music could you find?[8]

Luther's great contribution to the Protestant Reformation was his translation of the Scriptures from the original Greek and Hebrew languages of the

Bible into the German vernacular. But he did not stop with the Scriptures. Luther wanted hymns and songs to be accessible to the common people, too, and his first publication of songs, the Neue geistliche Gesänge of 1523, was written with four-part harmonization. This encouraged the singers to pay attention not only to the words of the song but also to its musical arrangement.

From 1600 to 1800, the world was introduced to the musical talents of Mozart, Bach, Handel and others who, through their masterful compositions, represent the peak of musical accomplishment. Works like Handel's *Messiah* and Bach's *Crucifixus* center on the fundamental teachings of the Christian faith. Bach even went so far as to sign each work *soli deo gloria* (to God alone be the glory).

The Puritan tradition, reacting against the Church of England and its use of the Book of Common Prayer, was suspicious of anything musical and resorted to the exclusive singing of the psalms. In 1644, it was recommended that "in the singing of psalms, the voice is to be tunably and gravely ordered; but the chief care must be to sing with understanding, and with grace in the heart, making melody unto the Lord."[9] Charles Haddon Spurgeon, the last of the great Puritans, understood their singular devotion, and he expressed his own passion for praising God:

> Do we sing as much as the birds do? Yet what have birds to sing about, compared with us? Do we sing as much as the angels do? Yet they were never redeemed by the blood of Christ. Bird of the air, shall you excel me? Angels, shall you exceed me? You have done so, but I intend to emulate you, and day by day, and night by night, pour forth my soul in sacred song.[10]

North America gave birth to a rich genre of Christian music. The journey from Africa to America was difficult for the slaves, but they did not hang their harps on the poplars (Psalm 137:2). "[The slaves on the ship] sang songs of sad lamentation. . . . They sang songs expressive of their fears of being beat, of their want of victuals, particularly the want of their native food, and of their never returning to their own country."[11] After several generations in America, the Africans embraced Christianity and flavored it with their own unique elements of worship, thus creating the Negro spiritual. Most slaves were uneducated and worked on plantations, and their hymns were seasoned with suffering, sorrow and an anticipation that they would soon be delivered from their bondage.

Like Taizé chants, Negro spirituals used simple, earthy language and often had no more than one or two stanzas:

> I want Jesus to walk with me,
> I want Jesus to walk with me,
> All along my pilgrim journey,
> I want Jesus to walk with me.[12]

These sacred songs reflect the struggles of slavery and the quest for equality; yet at the same time they esteem the presence and power of Jesus as the exalted God who gives grace to those in need.

Throughout the history of God's people, the Christian journey has incorporated the practice of praising God. While musical forms of worship are manifested in many ways—from Gregorian chant to Negro spirituals to classical sonatas—their theocentric focus unites them as a sacred expression of the Christian experience.

Taizé worship is spreading throughout the world. Churches are becoming more aware of its unique style, emphasis on silence and simple melodies. While Taizé worship continues to resonate with me, I have learned to worship in all kinds of environments. Worship is not limited to style, song or sanctuary; it is a way of life that incorporates the entire spectrum of saints. When we sing hymns to God, we do not sing them as isolated soloists performing on our own; rather, we stand side by side in the great choir of Christians who in the past have lifted their voices to Jesus Christ and worshiped him as the King of kings and the Lord of lords.

Lead gently, Lord, and slow
for fear that I may fall;
I know not where to go
unless I hear thy call.
My fainting soul doth yearn
for thy green hills afar;
so let thy mercy burn—
my greater, guiding star!

PAUL LAURENCE DUNBAR (1895)

BREAKING BREAD
WITH THE BENEDICTINES

Heavenly Hospitality

*As our lives and faith progress, the heart expands and with
the sweetness of love we move down the paths of God's commandments.*

THE RULE OF SAINT BENEDICT

Subiaco, Italy, A.D. 500

Benedict inhaled the sweet forest air. Mountain water trickled between his
toes. *At last,* he thought, *a quiet place for me to pray.*

Born into a wealthy family in Nursia, Italy, in 480, Benedict's parents
sent him to Rome to study literature and the liberal arts. But the secularism,
vulgarity and profligacy of urban Roman life wasn't his cup of tea. He pre-
ferred the wilderness—the chirping birds, the chanting owls, the smell of
sap, the shade of trees. Benedict sought separation, and in his solitude, he
found God.

But he also found Romanus, a monk who lived in a nearby monastery.
One day, while Benedict was fellowshiping with God on the summit of a
mountain, Romanus saw him praying. Romanus led him to an isolated cave
near his monastery, and every day he attached a piece of bread to the end of
a cord and lowered it down for Benedict to eat. For three years he did this,
making provisions for the young holy man.

Prayer, fasting and meditation filled Benedict's time. It was a hard life, a life of survival, difficulty and necessity. Yet it was a simple life, uncomplicated, a life of spiritual discovery and blessing. It was the life of most sixth-century monks who fled to the wilderness to escape the evils of the city. And Benedict wasn't entirely alone. God sent him a raven to be an earthly companion while he was engaged in heavenly transaction.

For three years Benedict lived alone. Soon his popularity became so great that he acquired a following of disciples. A group of young hermits visited Benedict's cave and insisted that he become the father of a local monastery called Vicovaro. The abbot of Vicovaro had just died, and the whole community believed that Benedict would naturally fill his place. Benedict was hesitant to accept the position because he loved his sacred solitude, but reluctantly he accepted the job. "Let me warn you," Benedict told them. "My monastic disciplines will be too extreme for you." The young men laughed and led him away, eager to have him as their spiritual leader, teacher and abbot.

Silence filled the room. It had been only several weeks since Benedict took the position, but the young hermits wanted him dead. Since talking was not permitted at the dinner table, the air was thick with tension. Father Benedict ate his meager meal while the students hurled death stares in his direction. He had been right all along—the disciplines were too grueling for the group. They could no longer tolerate the severe austerity; they had tried for weeks to kill him, but none of their conspiracies came to fruition. There was only one more thing to do.

Poison. Father Benedict would never see it coming. While one of the monks approached the father with a cup of wine in his hands, the others kept their eyes to the ground, hiding their smiles. Benedict reached for the cup. At last, the difficult days would be over. The rule was far too rough, and soon it would end. The anticipation was overwhelming. It was Benedict's custom to make the sign of the cross over his cup before drinking, so he raised his hand and proceeded to do so. Suddenly the cup, unable to contain its poisonous plot, exploded into a thousand little pieces. Shards of glass flew at the monks, who shielded themselves from the sharp missiles.

"May God Almighty have pity on you, my brothers," Benedict said. "Why do you wish to do this to me? Did I not say to you at the beginning that your ways and mine were incompatible? Go and seek an abbot for yourselves who suits your ways, because after this you definitely cannot have me." Their assassination attempt had been thwarted, and Father Benedict immediately left the monastery to once again embrace his beloved isolation.

He did not remain in his cave for long. In that day, most monks retreated by themselves into the hills to live a life of prayer and solitude. However, Benedict discovered that monasticism did not have to be so individualistic; he saw that these zealous, straying monks could live together in a community and worship God with one another. Although Benedict loved his isolation, he decided to marry his austere spirituality with the needs of the contemporary culture. After establishing twelve thriving monastic communities at Subiaco, Benedict wrote a manual for them that covered the nuts and bolts of monastic living.

It is called the Rule of Saint Benedict. Emphasizing prayer and work, the Rule is extremely pragmatic and sensible, explaining every aspect of monastic life: how to pray, when to talk, how to discipline, what to eat and so on. It is joyously overflowing with biblical insights and allusions, underscoring Benedict's own devotion to the Holy Scriptures. In essence, his writings were an extension of his passion to pull monasticism out of the sands of the desert and place it in the streets of the city. For the first time in European history, Christians could retreat to a Benedictine monastery to work, pray and defeat the devil in their own personal lives.

Over the centuries, the Rule of Saint Benedict gave shape, structure and identity to monastic communities. Gone were the days when a monk was forced to flee into the wilderness to seek a life of holiness. Benedictine Christianity offered another option—an option that gave stability and strength to a body of Christ that was still experiencing early growing pains.

Benedict died around 547 at Monte Cassino, but his words have not disappeared. Today there are more than fourteen hundred Benedictine communities filled with men and women who seek a more meaningful and spiritual way of life. Millions of people who seek a more simple life read the Rule of Saint Benedict. Kathleen Norris, an award-winning poet and bestselling author, says, "Over and over, the Rule calls us to be more mindful of the little things, even as it reminds us of the big picture, allowing us a glimpse of who we can be when we remember to love."[1]

The Benedictine way of life is a calling into deeper devotion to God and selfless communal living. Cloistered Christianity is certainly not for everyone. But for the monks who turn their backs on the pursuit of earthly advancement and fill their hours with prayer, work and study, their lives become mirrors reflecting the Christ who calls us to take our convictions a little more seriously and pursue with greater purpose the task of holy living.

Glenstal Abbey, County Limerick, Ireland, 2002

I sat down at the table with the Benedictine monks. They were wearing robes; I was wearing jeans. They were wise and resolved; I was antsy and squirming. If the Rule of Saint Benedict did not dictate mandatory mealtime silence, I would have been the first to spark the conversation. I might have opened with a joke, a story or a question about Irish monasticism.

Back home, mealtimes were talk times. They were times of informational exchange, intellectual confrontation and sometimes even heated debate. But this was not my culture and I was far from home. I was just a pilgrim finding hospitality in a monastery. The monks of Glenstal Abbey had gone out of their way to host me, and the least I could do was keep my mouth shut at the dinner table. How hard could it be?

Extremely hard! For an American who can talk a mile a minute, being silent required unparalleled discipline, concentration and willpower. *Awkward* gained a fresh new meaning for me at that table, but only for me. The monks sitting to my right and left were seasoned for the silence; they were creatures of prayer, inwardness and transparency. They did not share my inward struggle with silence nor the urge to make themselves heard. Like Saint Benedict, they were friends with the quiet, and when I looked at them, I knew I was experiencing something ancient.

The first dish was bread. With gracious smiles the monks passed it to me. Benedictine monks are known for their hospitality, but only when I arrived at Glenstal Abbey did I discover just how kind and hospitable they actually are.

We had come from Iona, Scotland. My adventure with the mud pit had ruined my tennis shoes, and if stains were scars, my clothes had bragging rights! To my surprise, a gentle-hearted monk named Patrick Lyons embraced my father and me and washed our clothes and shoes by hand. I was absolutely floored. Oh, the sour, mildewed stench he must have smelled! Oh, the gobs of Iona mud he must have seen! Never had man or monk displayed such "Jesus-ness" to me in all my life, and over the years my friendship with Father Lyons has become something I immensely treasure and enjoy.

Founded in 1927, Glenstal Abbey is a five-hundred-acre estate surrounded by lakes, woodlands and paths. Only about twelve miles from Limerick, the abbey can be reached by taxi from the bus or train station. A castle built in the romantic Norman style immediately captures the attention of the arriving pilgrim. At first its thick walls and round towers feel imposing, but when its gates open and its buildings embrace the traveler, the warm hospitality of the brethren quickly dissolves any intimidation the exterior might have produced.

Dedicated to Saints Joseph and Columba, Glenstal Abbey is a community of fifty monks who pray five times a day in the church, participating in the divine office and the mass. Pilgrims are welcome to attend these worship services, and those who do so find the singing of the modified grail Psalter of Gregorian chant both worshipful and engaging.

The monks in this community give themselves to work and prayer. They manage a boarding school for boys, a farm and guest services, and they involve themselves in pastoral and scholarly activities. They are environmentally conscious, having completed a wetland system to treat domestic and agricultural waste materials. The abbey also hosts educational seminars on energy resources and waste management. As part of its ongoing development, Glenstal houses a theological library of fifty-eight thousand books,

Irish manuscripts and archived items. Distance learning and adult education courses are also conducted within its walls.

The second dish of the meal put a smile on my face. It was more than bread but less than meat—it was vegetables. Pushing my craving for barbecue ribs and steak to the side, I picked up my utensils, surveyed the options and loaded my plate with humble portions of potatoes, beans and greens. I found it interesting that Benedictine monks do not eat large quantities of meat. Saint Benedict lived in a world in which everything was dualistically categorized as either spirit or flesh. According to this system of thought, eating the meat of four-legged creatures heightened the animalistic barbarism in the depraved human nature, so it was avoided.

Brother Terence dug in, cutting up his vegetables with great systematic resolve. First went the carrots, then the tomatoes, then the potatoes. All that silence rotated the wheels of my imagination, and I began to wonder what the monks were thinking about. Brother Terence looked deep in thought, and I studied him. I wondered if he dissected his theology like he dissected his food. With every stroke of his silverware, was he contemplating the deep mysteries of God? With every cut of his knife, could he be isolating the heresies of humanity?

Perhaps. The choice between broccoli and bread troubled him, but perhaps it was deeper than that. Perhaps it was a great dialogue between Catholics and Protestants, and the winner would be awarded first place in his mouth. Perhaps he was repeating the Psalter in his head or tracing the Sermon on the Mount in his mind. Perhaps mealtime in Glenstal Abbey meant more than just food; perhaps it meant thought and prayer as well.

Perhaps Brother Terence was dialoguing with God, working out his salvation with fear and trembling. Perhaps he was fending off demons and fighting off devils. Perhaps he was enjoying the silent moment without words to distract him or noise to deter him. Perhaps. But most likely he was just wondering why the young Baptist boy sitting across the table was staring at him. I smiled and looked away, as if I had my own thoughts to think. Oh, the awkwardness!

I don't recall the contents of the third dish, but I do remember the panic that plagued me when it was taken away. What was I going to do now? How was I going to avoid the virus of silence trying to infect me? At least the food had kept my mind alert and my mouth occupied. Now what? Would we just look at each other and pretend to be content? Would we exchange happy glances in hopes of talking later?

Yes. That's exactly the way it went. I wanted to talk of Luther and the Reformers, of Catholicism and Calvin. I wanted to hear their views on justification by faith alone, baptism and the holy Communion. My faith needed challenging; the paradoxes of my Protestantism needed resolving. But how could such a conversation occur when all was silent except the occasional clanging of silverware?

There would be other times for ecumenical dialogue. History is full of committees and councils where Protestants and Catholics have dialogued—but not today, not at this meal, not with these monks. The moment was made for silence. So there I sat, breaking bread with the Benedictines, learning the art of inner stillness and quietly fellowshiping with a table of my fellow Christians. The silence became sacred to me until I realized that gravy had been on my chin the whole time.

HEAVENLY HOSPITALITY

His pilgrimage had been a hard one. The prodigal son leaned against the pig trough, wondering how things had ended so badly for him. He remembered loading all his daddy's fortune in the bed of the pick-up truck and driving away to the city. He remembered how fun it was to cruise the crowds, deal the drugs and play the pimp. He was one bad dog. But apparently God was holding the keys to the kennel and he was about to snatch that dog up by its leash. A famine fell on the city, forcing the prodigal into the pigpen.

It's hard to start out in the palace and end up in the prison. The prodigal son looked over at the food the pigs were eating. It looked nothing like his mama's sweet apple pie! His fancy china had become a wooden trough, and he longed for grandma's good cooking. The nostalgic scent of heaven had become the awful smell of hell, and there he was, a young Jewish boy sitting with unclean animals. Life doesn't get much lower. *How many of my father's hired men have food to spare,* the prodigal son wondered, *and here I am starving to death!*

Perhaps the prodigal learned a lesson living in the pigpen. When God said to himself, *I will make a pig,* he did not bless it with the power he bestowed on the bull. Nor did he give the pig an Einstein of an intellect, capable of reasoning through its little schedule. But the same God who feeds the fish of a thousand waves and clothes the lilies of a thousand hills provides warm pods for his pigs when they oink for their dinner.

The prodigal son scratched his head. *I am not a pig,* he thought, *but neither am I a son any longer. Perhaps if I were a slave, my father would feed me and let me back inside his house.*

With a growl in his stomach and a heavy step, the prodigal pilgrim went home. While he was still a great distance away, something surfaced on the horizon.

Oh no, he thought. *It's my father's servants, sent to beat me.*

He looked closer.

Or perhaps my brother, sent to scold me.

He squinted.

Maybe it's just a fatted calf, wandering away from its herd.

Suddenly, the prodigal son stopped dead in his tracks and rubbed his eyes. *It's my father.*

From a mile away the father recognized the face of his little boy. He saw the dirt on his clothes and the pods in his hair, but that didn't matter. Nothing, in fact, mattered at the moment. He had spent many nights waiting on the front porch for his son to return, but every dot in the distance turned out to be a goat or camel, lost in the desert. This time it was different. This time it was for real. Like an Olympic athlete racing for the prize, the father sprinted out to greet his prodigal pilgrim.

Hospitality is a necessary element of pilgrimage, and Matthew captured the spirit of it in his Gospel:

Come, you who are blessed by my Father; take your inheritance, the kingdom prepared for you since the creation of the world. For I was hungry and you gave me something to eat, I was thirsty and you gave me something to drink, I was a stranger and you invited me in. (Matthew 25:34-35)

In the ancient Near East, hospitality was offered to complete strangers. Since people often had to travel through enemy territory, hospitality to strangers was a matter of survival. In Genesis 18, Abraham and his wife Sarah offered hospitality to three strangers who turned out to be angels. In keeping with this idea, the author of Hebrews commands his readers, "Do not forget to entertain strangers, for by so doing some people have entertained angels without knowing it" (Hebrews 13:2). Both Jewish and Christian traditions emphasize hospitality as a predominant teaching and fundamental practice. Saint Benedict wrote in his Rule, "All guests to the monastery should be welcomed as Christ."[2] Benedictine monasticism takes seriously the calling to be kind, gracious and compassionate to strangers because in dealing with them, they are dealing with Jesus Christ himself.

Sharing a meal has become a universal expression of hospitality. Theologian Alexander Schmemann notes, "Centuries of secularism have failed to transform eating into something strictly utilitarian. Food is still treated with reverence."[3] Not only is food treated with reverence, but eating together is also a symbol of a solid friendship. This is why Paul warns the church at Corinth that "you must not associate with anyone who calls himself a brother but is sexually immoral or greedy, an idolater or a slanderer, a drunkard or a swindler. With such a man do not even eat" (1 Corinthians 5:11).

I did not know the true meaning of hospitality until I went to Glenstal Abbey. Upon arrival, my stomach had been upset for several days. Noticing this, Father Lyons and his fellow monks went to their garden and picked several apples for me to eat. It was perhaps the turning point of my pilgrimage. As I sank my teeth into the sweet flesh of the apple, I was reminded that hospitality is nothing more than treating strangers like they are Jesus. To this day, I cannot even invite a guest to my apartment for dinner without remembering how Benedictine monasticism welcomed and fed me. It is a contagious kind of Christianity.

The silence that I struggled to maintain at the table plagued me throughout the remainder of my time at the abbey. But each meal became a little easier. When I sat down beside the brothers my compulsion to communicate decreased, and I discovered that observing silence in this monastic setting was a way that I could demonstrate hospitality to them in turn. The lack of words communicated my respect and admiration for their way of life more completely than an hour of dialogue. Esther de Waal writes, "Here again is the paradox, that by emptying myself I am not only able to give but also to receive. Filled with prejudice, worry, jealousy, I have no inner space to listen, to discover the gift of the other person, to take down my defenses and be open to what they have to offer."[4]

The prodigal son had to empty himself of pride before he could return to his father. He had to learn the secrets of the pigpen before he could appreciate the luxuries of the mansion. As he arrived home, the father threw his arms around his boy, put a ring on his finger and ordered a large feast. At last the waiting was over. The son who once was lost was found, and the fattest of the cattle was slaughtered in his honor.

The parable of the prodigal son parallels our own journey to God. In our rebellion we have strayed from Eden and squandered our inheritance in the city. But God is not content to let us wander in this wilderness; he is running out to greet us, and we are traveling to our second and final Eden. In his book *The Return of the Prodigal Son,* Henri Nouwen writes:

> God is not the patriarch who stays at home, doesn't move, and expects his children to come to him, apologize for their aberrant behavior, beg for forgiveness, and promise to do better. To the contrary, he leaves the house, ignoring his dignity by running toward them, pays no heed to apologies and promises of change, and brings them to the table richly prepared for them.[5]

Jesus once told his disciples, "In my Father's house are many rooms; if it were not so, I would have told you. I am going there to prepare a place for you" (John 14:2). With that in mind, the wealth of this world can no longer satisfy us, and though we temporarily reside in the pigpen, as strangers and aliens we travel home to our father who embraces us, forgives us and welcomes us not as slaves but as sons and daughters. We are indeed recipients of divine grace and victims of unconditional love.

Almighty God,
By whose grace St. Benedict,
Kindled with the fire of your love,
became a burning and a shining light in the church:
inflame us with the same spirit
of discipline and love,
that we may walk before you
as children of light;
through Jesus Christ our Lord.

ESTHER DE WAAL

A GLIMPSE OF GLORY

The Path of Worship

One of the great blessings of heaven is the appreciation of heaven on earth.
He is no fool who gives what he cannot keep to gain what he cannot lose.

JIM ELLIOT

Palm Beach, Ecuador, January 8, 1956

With lances in hand and hatred in heart, the Waodani Indians emerged from the dense jungle foliage. The tribe was known for murdering outsiders, and even though the five American missionaries were likely shouting "Puinani! Puinani!" ("Welcome! Welcome!"), a blur of spears and sand covered the scene. Jim Elliot and his friends had brought along handguns in case things got out of hand, but they knew that killing a Waodani would eliminate their chances of reaching the Amazon tribe for Christ. So instead, they engaged the naked warriors with kindness.

Born in Portland, Oregon, Jim Elliot became a Christian at the age of eight. His father was an itinerant evangelist and his mother conducted a chiropractic practice. During his early life, missionaries visited his home and told stories of distant cultures and faraway places. These young years proved pivotal for Jim, not only because they exposed him to the work of foreign missionaries but also because they formed in him a deep sensitivity to God's workings in other regions of the world.

He attended Benson Polytechnic High School and studied architectural drawing. His athletic skills landed him on the football field, and his wrestling skills drove him to the mat. Acting became second nature, and his teachers were so impressed with his performances that they insisted he enter a professional theater.

But Jim Elliot had a burden to preach. He loved sharing God's Word with God's people. Gradually, he moved from the drawing table to the preaching pulpit, and in 1945 he became a student at Wheaton College to become better equipped for his calling. Greek and Hebrew were difficult to learn, but his passion for understanding the Scriptures in their original languages urged him onward. He soon developed a passion for reaching unreached people groups, and his calling to become a missionary to South America solidified. He was driven by the realization that while there was one Christian worker for every five hundred people in the United States, there was one for every fifty thousand in foreign lands.

In 1948, Jim was elected president of the Foreign Mission Fellowship, and during this time he began journaling. He practiced this discipline with great devotion, and his entries reveal a keen awareness of God's presence. In an entry written on July 7, 1948, Jim reflected, almost prophetically, on Psalm 104:4: "[God] makest the winds thy messengers, fire and flame thy ministers" (KJV). The devotional reads, "Am I ignitable? God deliver me from the dread asbestos of 'other things.' Saturate me with the oil of the Spirit that I may be a flame. But flame is transient, often short-lived."[1] Jim Elliot poured his life into his journals, and the flame that burned in his heart drove him deep into the jungles of the Amazon rainforest.

Before he left, however, he met a young woman named Elisabeth Howard. Born in Belgium, Elisabeth attended Wheaton College to study classical Greek. During Jim's junior year at school, they fell in love. Though Elisabeth was academically a year ahead, spiritually they were on the same plane. Both sought to serve the Lord on the mission field, and the opportunity arose in 1952. Jim and his friend Ed McCully sailed to Quito, Ecuador, and stayed with a missionary family in preparation for his ministry to the

Waodani. For six months they gained a working knowledge of Spanish, tropical diseases and useful medicines. Elisabeth later joined him in Ecuador, and in October of 1953, they were married. After their daughter, Valerie, was born, Jim and Elisabeth worked to translate the New Testament into the Waodani language.

The Waodani, also known as Huaorani, Waorani or Auca (meaning "savage"), were an indigenous tribe of about two thousand people in the Amazon region. Located between the Curaray and Napo rivers about fifty miles south of Dureno, Ecuador, the remote tribe was used to protecting its land from foreign invaders they called *cowode* (literally "nonhuman cannibals"). Motivated by fear, curiosity and warfare, killing had become a sport for them—a way of life both within and without the boundaries of the tribe. Around the time of World War II, 60 percent of the tribe had been murdered as a result of revenge and interclan hostilities.

The forest protected the Waodani from neighboring peoples and cultures that threatened their existence. Their land was about 120 miles wide and 100 miles from north to south. They strongly believed that there was no difference between the physical and spiritual worlds, and thus they had no word for *God*, only words for *demon* and *spirit*. They ritualistically worshiped animals and believed that the spirits who failed to enter the domain of the dead would reincarnate in the next life as animals.

This belief, however, did not hinder the tribe from hunting. Having mastered the spear and blowgun, the Waodani hunted all kinds of animals. Since the eye of a deer is similar to the eye of a human, though, they did not eat deer meat. Anacondas and jaguars were also prohibited since they were considered fundamentally evil. But they hunted monkeys, wild peccaries and birds with great vigor and violence.

Against this primitive background, Jim and Elisabeth Elliot ventured into the swamplands of Waodani territory. Four missionaries and their wives accompanied them: Ed McCully, Roger Youderian, Peter Fleming and pilot Nate Saint. Together they built a temporary mission station, a medical building, living quarters and an airstrip, but a ferocious rainy season soon destroyed their camp.

The first contact with the Indians occurred when Jim and his friends discovered Waodani huts when flying in the plane. They shouted friendly words in the Waodani language and dropped a basket of gifts including cloth, beads, hamburgers and photographs in hopes of establishing a friendly relationship with the tribe. After four months of this, the Waodani allowed them to land their plane. The group set down on the banks of the Curaray River and called the landing strip Palm Beach. On numerous occasions, curious Indians approached them, and the men's spirits were high that evangelism would soon become a realistic option. After four days of living on the beach, two Indians befriended them. The missionaries named them George and Delilah. Operation Waodani seemed to be a great success.

On January 8, thirty Waodani men were spotted heading toward Palm Beach. The five missionaries were excited, and Jim reported the event to Elisabeth over a two-way radio, saying, "We'll call you back in three hours." Elisabeth and the other wives prayed earnestly for their husbands' safety. They expected to hear from them again at 4:30 p.m., and they turned the radio on. They looked at the clock. "Any word from Palm Beach?" they asked into the transmitter. Silence. Five minutes. Ten minutes. Something was wrong. They would not let themselves entertain the terrible thought, but secretly they feared the worst. The hollow crackle of silence mocked their racing imaginations.

Helicopters from the Ecuadorian Air Force flew over the banks of the Curaray River. A search team was issued. Several days later, the women received word that a body had been found floating facedown in the water. Then another and another and another. Nate Saint's watch was recovered. It had stopped at 3:12 p.m.—the likely moment of their murders. Five bodies were recovered and laid on the beach, having been violently mutilated with spears and machetes. Even the plane had been torn to pieces by the weapons of the warriors. For the five missionaries, the Curaray River became the Jordan, and the martyrs courageously journeyed to the other side.

Grief came in waves. The five women were in the kitchen when they received the news of their husbands' deaths. They tried to imagine the scene:

"Which of the men watched the others fall? Which of them had time to think of his wife and children? Had one been covering the others in the tree house, and come down in an attempt to save them? Had they suffered long?"[2] There were no answers for these widows, but the fact that not a single Waodani was injured during the violent encounter bears testimony to the martyrs' love and calling to the selfless task of evangelism.

The story doesn't end there. The widows did not believe their husbands had died in vain, so they continued their missionary work with the Waodani. Pursuing revival instead of revenge, Elisabeth and her daughter, Valerie, met her husband's murderers and worked courageously for their salvation.

The Waodani have embraced Christianity, and many have now been converted. While Jim Elliot and his friends cannot enjoy the rich bounty of their missions work, they gave the lives they could not keep to gain the God they could not lose. Five years before his death, Jim wrote these words in his journal: "I sensed afresh last evening the truth of Paul's words, 'How shall they preach, except they be sent?' Oh God, here I am, send me. Let me not miss my path in running ahead. Send me, oh, send me afield!"[3]

Amsterdam, July 29, 2000

It was a hint of heaven, a foretaste of the kingdom of God. More than eleven thousand Christians from two hundred countries congregated in Amsterdam for the Billy Graham conference. More nations came together for this Christian event than are represented in the United Nations.

It was a pilgrimage of epic proportion. Hundreds came by foot, camel and bike. Some came from Africa, having sold their cows to purchase the plane ticket. Others came from Asia, having traveled by boat and barge. Hotels and hostels were packed with pilgrims. Buses and taxis were flooded with foreigners. No one wanted to miss the conference that would stir the city and shake the world.

Designed to equip and encourage pastors, missionaries and evangelists, the Amsterdam 2000 conference attracted thousands of people of every race, tongue and tribe. The corridors of the complex swarmed with pilgrims. It was as if the entire body of Christ had been sewn together before my very eyes. Capillaries of Christians were united; arteries of evangelists were connected; and as the sinews of saints were attached, I realized that if the body of Christ had ever been dismembered, surely it was not now. Here in sin-saturated Amsterdam, the world would watch the church be the church. And I braced for impact.

Due to illness, Billy Graham could not attend, but his opening words were sent by satellite to us:

> You are gathered in Amsterdam from over two hundred countries. You may have traveled thousands of miles and at great sacrifice to be here tonight. But why are you all there in that beautiful city? What is the purpose of all the planning, the work, the travel, and price that we have paid? We have come together to discover how the evangelical Church worldwide can further the Kingdom of God by the proclamation of the Gospel.[4]

Attending the conference were Christian thinkers, theologians, writers and speakers who in their unique ways contributed to the growth and building up of the body of Christ. Some of the greatest evangelical leaders of the twentieth century attended: John Stott, J. I. Packer, Chuck Colson, Billy Kim, Paul Finkenbinder, Stephen Olford, Bill Bright, Antoine Rutayisire, Sami Dagher, Ravi Zacharias, Dennis Rainey, Philemon Choi, Uwe Holmer, Josh McDowell, Archbishop of Canterbury George Carey, Ajith Fernando, Tokunboh Adeyemo, Ulrich Parzany, Anne Graham Lotz and Franklin Graham, among others.

The opening ceremony evoked great enthusiasm from the audience. Sitting beside David Riker and my father, I looked across the auditorium, soaking up the eschatology of it all. Countless flags were flying. Dozens of languages were being spoken. It was a world of diversity beneath a roof of commonality, and I thought of John's vision on the isle of Patmos:

> After this I looked and there before me was a great multitude that no one could count, from every nation, tribe, people and language,

standing before the throne and in front of the Lamb. They were wearing white robes and were holding palm branches in their hands. And
they cried out in a loud voice:

> "Salvation belongs to our God,
> who sits on the throne,
> and to the Lamb." (Revelation 7:9-10)

During the service, Cliff Barrows invited each person to pray aloud in
his or her own native tongue. Bowing my head, I prayed the Lord's Prayer,
but I'll never forget the sounds surrounding me. It was chaotic yet somehow unified—a mixture of tongues and languages unlike anything I had
ever heard.

After the worship service, everyone poured into the halls of the enormous
complex. Walking along I met dozens of pastors and missionaries and ran
into people I'd only read about in books.

As I turned the corner, I saw a man holding what looked like a spear. Intrigued, I approached him. His clothes were tribal and his face inviting. His
leathered arms were covered with tattoos and his ears were pierced with
large circles. On his mouth was a smile and on his head a fur hat. I didn't
know if he spoke English, but I attempted a conversation anyway.

"Hello, my name's Christian."

He smiled but did not say a word.

"His name is Mincaye Enquedi Huahue," an interpreter provided. "And
my name is Steve Saint."

"Steve Saint?" I asked. "Was your father Nate Saint?"

He nodded. "That's right. The man beside me is the Indian who killed
him. Mincaye became a Christian and has come to Amsterdam to tell the
global church that he is sorry for his crime."

I looked at his red, black and yellow-tipped spear. It was slender and
sharp, laced with rope and color. Perhaps this was the last thing Jim Elliot
and his friends saw on that sandy riverbank nearly fifty years ago. I tried to
imagine the way it went—the yells, the wounds, the struggle, the cries for

peace, the deaths. How terrified those five missionaries must have been to see those spears!

Sticking out my hand, I greeted Mincaye. He shook it firmly. I could see repentance in his eyes—years of regret and remorse. How many times had he turned the memory of his murders over in his mind? A hundred? A thousand? Maybe a million? I felt for him and wanted to let him know the fullness of Christ's forgiveness. I wanted to speak to him in his own language, the language Jim Elliot and Nate Saint learned, but instead I simply patted him on the shoulder and welcomed him into the body of Christ.

Midway through the week, I had a memorable experience in the dining hall. Volunteers from more than thirty-five countries were serving about 385,000 people, and I picked up my meal and sat down. It included a sandwich, an apple, some crackers and a bottle of water. Several Romanian pastors sat with me at my table. They told me of their struggles through the years and of how many of their friends had been martyred during the days of Communism. I told them of my pilgrimage to Hungry, Romania and Russia, and about the men and women I knew who had suffered tremendous cruelty at the hands of the Communists. Although their accents were thick, we learned a lot about one another.

Before the iron grip of Communism had lifted from Romania, Christians had to worship beneath the cloak of secrecy. Bibles were burned, Christians were killed and persecution ravaged the church. In those days, being a Christian was a costly thing. Often soldiers broke into the home of a Christian family and shot the family members one by one, leaving only the children to remember the high price of bearing the name of Christ.

In one Romanian village, a group of Christians refused to let their faith be defused; they smuggled a Bible into their village. If discovered, they would face death, but they were willing to take that risk. Since the village had only one Bible, each family tore a page from it and committed it to memory. After savoring every word, learning every line and internalizing every story, the pages were burned and the evidence destroyed.

Every week those families came together to worship God in one of their

homes. Disguised as a simple meal, these dinners were a time of spiritual refreshment and encouragement. Each family shared with the others the content of their pages. Some had a page from Genesis, others from Amos, others
from Daniel, and still others from Luke. Meal by meal, month by month,
year by year, the Christians of that Romanian village absorbed the truth of
the Bible one page at a time, and eventually they covered the entire spectrum
of the Scriptures. The body of Christ, though in hiding, was nourished,
healthy and growing.

Each time I think about that story, a fresh wave of conviction sweeps over
me. I come from a land where Bibles pour from our ears—a dime a dozen
in every translation, version, color, size and shape. Big print, small print,
thin pages, thick pages. Some come in cowhide, others come in alligator
leather. Some come with Velcro, others come with beads.

The Romanian pastors finished their story, and I imagined how overwhelming it must have been for a Romanian Christian to hold not only one
page of the Bible but the whole holy thing! How precious to scan from
Joshua to James, from Ezekiel to Ephesians, from Romans to Revelation. The
Scriptures must have been so sacred to them, so priceless! I got up from that
meal embarrassed that the Bibles sitting on my shelves at home suffered
from dust and neglect. And I wondered if there would be enough evidence
to convict me if Christianity became illegal in America.

The Scriptures are an essential element of the Christian tradition. The
Amsterdam 2000 conference upheld the importance of the Word of God by
organizing three special task forces of theologians, church leaders and strat-
egists who sought to equip Christians across the world with the necessary
tools to face the problems of the upcoming century. We came to the conference because my father was asked to be the chairman of the drafting com-
mittee for the theological task group. Their responsibility involved writing
The Amsterdam Declaration, a document that outlined the essential claims
and fundamental truths of the evangelical Christian tradition.

At the end of the conference, all attendees were invited to raise their right
hands and pledge to commit themselves to this document. It encouraged

them to embrace "the truth of the gospel and to carry out with faithfulness the calling God had placed on their lives."[5] Part of the pledge read, "We pledge ourselves to keep the Scriptures at the very heart of our evangelistic outreach and message, and to remove all language and cultural barriers to a clear understanding of the gospel on the part of our hearers."[6] At the end of the conference, twenty-two plenary sessions had been translated into twenty-two languages, and dozens of practical workshops had prepared the body of Christ to engage the twenty-first century.

In one of the last worship services, Reverend Richard Bewes, pastor of All Souls Church in London, welcomed every believing Christian to participate in holy Communion. Thousands of bread pieces and cups of juice were distributed throughout the arena as we celebrated the Christian faith by obeying the Lord's command. It was a breathtaking banquet, a foretaste of heavenly fellowship, and though in this life we see only glimpses of glory, the Amsterdam 2000 convention reminded us that Christians will one day live together in harmony, and the church will dwell in unity for eternity.

MORE THAN DOUGHNUTS

When I was a teenager I went to church for all the wrong reasons. First of all, it was a great place to meet girls and show off some new clothes. The music and singing entertained me, and the holiest thing I talked about in Sunday school was the white powdered doughnut that drew me there.

But God wanted more. He wanted genuine worship and complete abandonment of my strong ego, selfish motives and materialistic attractions. To worship God is an act of total surrender. It requires us to yield everything to him—our words, wallets, dreams, desires, attitudes and ambitions. The God who lavishes us with love deserves to be lavished with praise, and when that happens, the Father's will is done on earth as it is in heaven.

Ecclesiology is the study of the church. What is the church called to be? What is its identity? How can the church be the church? The church is more than the walls of a sanctuary, more than a group of individuals who share a common cause. The church is a body of Christians who participate in genuine worship. This the heart of biblical ecclesiology.

In the Old Testament, God commanded his people to bring gifts, sacrifices and offerings to the temple as an outward manifestation of an inward
surrendering. Worship requires both a surrendering and a rendering. After
surrendering ourselves, we render our gifts to God; we bring him offerings
of humility and give him sacrifices of obedience. We soak him with showers
of adoration and honor him with songs of glory. This is the cream of the
Christian crop, the heartbeat of sacred worship, and at the end of the day,
God is ultimately interested not in what we can get out of church but in who
we encounter when sitting in the pew. J. I. Packer writes:

> The Puritans were concerned about communion with God in a way
> we are not. The measure of our unconcern is the little that we say
> about it. When Christians meet, they talk to each other about their
> Christian work and Christian interests, their Christian acquaintances,
> the state of the churches, and the problem of theology—but rarely of
> their daily experience of God.[7]

David wrote extensively about his experiences with God. The book of
Psalms is swollen with autobiographical information about how God rescued the needy and delivered the helpless. In the twenty-third Psalm, David
paints a picture of pilgrimage. He begins his journey in the pasture and travels to the temple via the valley. His journey is aimed at one thing—the worship of God.

In medieval times, pilgrims often trudged through dangerous ravines and
valleys of death. Plymouth pilgrims journeyed from England to America because they sought to worship God with freedom and liberty. Many who attempted the rough voyage across the Atlantic never emerged from the valley
of the shadow, and those who did were faced with the manifold hazards of
colonizing a new continent. Nevertheless, pilgrimage must find its center in
the worship of God.

Genuine worship revolves around Christ's pilgrimage from heaven back to
heaven via the depths of hell. God's glory is expressed in creation, revelation

and salvation, but it is most clearly seen in the resurrection of Jesus Christ. If Jesus' body were discovered in some Middle Eastern tomb, the Christian faith would be the biggest joke in all the world—a religion to be pitied, not propagated. But Christ has risen from the dead and ascended into heaven.

We place all our eggs in the Easter basket.

By keeping Christ's pilgrimage in the front of our minds, our worship lends itself to divine satisfaction, and with Jim Elliot we say, "Oh, the fullness, pleasure, sheer excitement of knowing God on earth."[8] The Amsterdam 2000 conference reminded me that "at the name of Jesus every knee should bow, in heaven and on earth and under the earth, and every tongue confess that Jesus Christ is Lord, to the glory of God the Father" (Philippians 2:10-11).

I have come to the conclusion that I may never play a clarinet like Benny Goodman, kick a soccer ball like Pelé, preach the gospel like Spurgeon, spark a reformation like Luther, paint a picture like Caravaggio, write a song like Gershwin, invent a martial art like Bruce Lee, convert the Irish like Saint Patrick or carve a sculpture like Michelangelo. But God does not require me to. He simply asks for genuine worship, simple obedience and consistent faithfulness.

Christians are not required to change the world; we're required to worship the God who changes the heart. In doing so, we follow his will. Sometimes it leads us into the depths of the jungle, other times to the heart of the sea. But no matter where his Spirit takes us, no matter where his hand directs us, we can be confident that the God who calls us by name will not forget us by accident, and his power and presence will always be with us, even "to the very end of the age" (Matthew 28:20).

Oh Lord, send me anywhere only go with me, lay any burden upon me only sustain me, and sever any tie that binds me except the tie that binds me to thy heart.

DAVID LIVINGSTON

ROAMING THROUGH ROME

The Journey Home

But in keeping with his promise we are looking forward to a
new heaven and a new earth, the home of righteousness.

2 PETER 3:13

Near the Circus of Caligula, Rome, A.D. 64

Peter struggled against the grain of the wood. He was an old man and it had been many years since he had seen Jesus. The hands that fished for men were now wrinkled and worn. The voice that preached the gospel was hoarse and sore. The feet that walked on water now supported the weight of his body as he hung upside down on a wooden cross in Rome.

"I tell you the truth," Jesus once said to Peter on the shore of Galilee. "When you were younger you dressed yourself and went where you wanted; but when you are old you will stretch out your hands, and someone else will dress you and lead you where you do not want to go" (John 21:18).

Jesus was right. Nero had set fire to Rome and accused the Christians of doing it. Massive persecution broke out and thousands of believers were martyred. As Peter hung on his cross, he thought he heard the crowing of a rooster in the distance. For years that noise had haunted him; he hated roosters. Wherever he was, their crowing jarred his ear. Peter never escaped the guilt of denying Jesus, and many nights had passed with tears streaming down his cheeks.

How wonderful it would have been, Peter thought, *if we had not abandoned our Lord at Golgotha! What an honor it would have been to die with Jesus!*

But it was far too late for those kinds of thoughts. Death was blinks away, and Peter's earthly pilgrimage had nearly ended. The roads of his life had led him to Rome, but soon he would take another journey—a journey to see Jesus once again, face to face.

St. Peter's Basilica, Rome, 1999

Every trip and travel had prepared us for Rome, the pinnacle of our pilgrimages. The three of us, David Riker, my father and I, sat behind the prime minister of Italy, directly under the decorated dome of Saint Peter's Basilica. Dozens of cardinals surrounded us, including Cardinal Joseph Ratzinger (now Pope Benedict XVI). Twenty thousand pilgrims sat and stood behind us, having come from all parts of the world to participate in the annual patron feast of Saints Peter and Paul. It was one of the biggest pilgrimages of the year, and the square of Saint Peter's was packed with people.

Pope John Paul II sat only feet from us, fraily conducting the morning mass. The years had taken their toll on him, but every now and then a flash of spirit burst across his face, and for a moment he was young again.

As the Latin hymns soothed me, I looked at the altar and the massive bronze baldachino spiraling upward toward Michelangelo's dome. I thought of all the pilgrims who had visited this sanctuary over the years. The stones beneath us had felt the feet of Luther, Bonhoeffer and hundreds of great leaders of the Christian faith. Rome has attracted literary giants like Goethe, Keats, Byron, the Brownings and Hans Christian Anderson. As I sat in amazement, absorbing its history, I came to appreciate what Catholicism has contributed to Christianity. While I have my own doctrinal and theological preferences (as did Luther), my eyes expanded beyond my denominational differences, and for the first time in my life, I felt grateful for the commonalities that I shared with my Catholic friends.

For several days we roamed through Rome. We climbed the Spanish Steps, saw the Trevi Fountain and ate Italian ice cream near the Colosseum.

We visited the Pantheon, Roman Forum, Trajan's column, the Arch of Titus, the church of Saint Maria di Loreto and the baths of Caracalla. Father Patrick Lyons of Ireland, whom we met for the first time here, took us to Trastevere, one of the oldest sections of Rome and the probable location of Peter's ministry. After eating a meal with the Benedictine brothers at San Anselmo, a religious university and community, we explored the musty catacombs beneath the city. Both Peter and Paul walked through Rome, and it was humbling to know that we were following in their footsteps.

Looking up at the ceiling of the basilica, I meditated on the words painted around the edge of the dome: *Tu es Petrus et super hance petrum aedificabo ecclesiam meam et tibi dabo claves regni caelorum* (You are Peter and upon this rock I will build my church and I will give to you the keys of the kingdom of heaven). According to church tradition, Simon Peter was martyred directly beneath where we sat. In A.D. 64, Nero accused the Christians of setting fire to Rome, and in retaliation he tortured and martyred many of them. According to Tacitus, "They were clothed in the skins of wild beasts, and torn to pieces by dogs; they were fastened to crosses, or set up to be burned so as to serve the purpose of lamps when daylight failed."[1]

Tradition holds that Peter was crucified upside down next to an Egyptian obelisk in the center of Caligula's circus, which ran beneath the basilica. Caligula's circus was a place of games and chariot races, but for Nero, this was a great location to demonstrate his wrath against the obscure Christian sect. After his death, Peter was placed in an undisclosed grave in a cemetery that adjoined the circus. The exact spot was known only to the persecuted Christians.

Three hundred years later, when Constantine legalized Christianity, he built a basilica across the Tiber River on Vatican Hill, directly above the grave of Peter. In the sixteenth century the structure was torn down, stone for stone, and what replaced it has evolved into Saint Peter's Basilica, the largest church in Christendom. Over the past seventeen hundred years, millions of people have visited the basilica to behold its beauty and marvel at its relics.

Now, I'm a serious skeptic of relics. I've seen enough pieces of Christ's cross to construct another Noah's ark. However, the evidence that Peter's bones were once beneath the basilica is quite compelling, and after the morning mass we were given tickets to go beneath Saint Peter's crypt and see for ourselves the famous *scavi,* or excavation.

The central aisle of Saint Peter's Basilica stretches roughly four hundred feet from the entrance to the altar. One level below lies the burial crypt, known as the Sacred Grottoes. But we were going deeper than that. On the outside of the basilica, an entrance took us into the *scavi.* Step by step we sank into the bowels of the basilica. The air grew cold, and we passed several archeological teams brushing dirt away from cracking tombstones and Roman roads. We walked through the rooms, passing ancient frescoes and pagan urns filled with cremated bodies. We were in an ancient cemetery! When Constantine built this church, he filled the graveyard with compacted dirt that inadvertently preserved the contents for future generations.

In February 1939, archeologists began excavations below the burial crypt. They removed the floor with sledgehammers and crowbars. When they struck dirt, they dug into the old soil with shovels. Then they struck brick. Brick walls began to surface, and eventually the walls formed buildings. Inside these buildings, they discovered pagan tombs and Roman urns. But then they exposed something unexpected. After removing almost six thousand cubic feet of earth, they found a marble slab with a carving of a woman about to draw water from a well. The Latin words *anima dulcis Gorgonia* (sweet-souled Gorgonia) were inscribed above it, along with the name Amelia Gorgonia. The archeologists were elated: Before them was the tomb of an early Christian woman.

In 1941, diggers discovered other Christian tombs. One of them bore the name Flavius Statilius Olympius. His inscription sheds light on the personal characteristics valued by New Testament Christians in Rome. It reads, "He had a joke for everyone and he never quarreled."[2] Could this man have been acting in obedience to Paul's letter to the Roman church? "If it is possible, as far as it depends on you, live at peace with everyone" (Romans 12:18).

The New Testament is silent about the death of Peter. Acts 12 records that Peter was almost killed by King Herod Agrippa I in Jerusalem. Wanting to please the Jews, Herod killed James, the brother of John, and arrested Peter. He ordered sixteen soldiers to guard him and threw him in prison, probably in the Tower of Antonia. After an angel rescued him, Peter went to Mark's house (this was a regular meeting place for Christians and possibly the place where Jesus and his disciples had the Last Supper).[3] He knocked on the door until Rhoda, a servant girl, recognized his voice and ran through the house telling everyone he had arrived. Thinking it was his angel, they opened the door and he told them what had happened. Then "he left for another place" (Acts 12:17).

As the archeological team continued to uncover tombs beneath the basilica, they discovered a sketch in Valerius's tomb. Two heads were outlined with red lead and charcoal. The upper was clearly the head of Christ in the form of the phoenix resurrecting from the ashes. Inscribed on its forehead was the Latin word *vibus* (living). The lower head revealed an older man, balding, with a wrinkled brow and a beard. Below it were the words "Peter pray Christ Jesus for the holy . . ."[4] The inscription mysteriously cuts off.

Moving beneath the area of the high altar, the archeologists then discovered four Christian mosaics. The first mosaic depicted Jonah falling from a ship, the second a fisherman, and the third a shepherd with a sheep in his arms. But the fourth proved most interesting. Part of the scene had been destroyed, but what remained was magnificent. A chariot drawn by two white horses pulled a bearded male whose right arm was raised and whose left arm held a globe. Behind his head shone rays of light, suggesting the form of the cross. Clearly they were staring at the Greek god Helios, adapted to the Christian portrayal of Christ.

We pressed on, following in the steps of the diggers, examining the faded Christian mosaics. I thought of past pilgrimages to the great cathedrals of England, the lofty prayer mountains of Korea, the towering castles of Europe and the icy fjords of Scandinavia. Somehow, every pilgrimage I had ever taken fell short in comparison to this one. I stepped carefully on the Roman road leading me deeper into the earth, knowing that each step brought me closer not only to Peter's grave but also to the climax of all my pilgrimages combined.

The archeologists, who were almost directly beneath the high altar, ran into a wall—literally. According to legend, Pope Anacletus ordered the construction of a small shrine over Peter's grave. In the year 200, Gaius referred to the "Tropaion" of Peter, standing on Vatican Hill.[5] Over this shrine, Constantine built his church. After breaching the shrine, the team discovered a wall with Christian names inscribed on it, complete with the Latin phrase *Vivatis in Christo* (May you live in Christ). Appearing at least thirty times was the chi-rho symbol—the first two Greek letters of Christ's name intertwined.

Having probed every angle of the shrine, the archeologists decided to dig beneath it. Peter must be close. At a depth of eighteen inches, a grave was discovered. The excavators were enthusiastic—but disappointed; it proved to be a grave from the fourth century. Deeper they dug. The lead archeologist, Engelbert Kirschbaum, suddenly found a recess in the wall. He reached inside and pulled back a bone. Trembling, he wondered if he might be holding a bone of Peter.

It was evening, but Pope Pius XII was summoned into the basilica to see the discovery. More bones were recovered from the recess, and after medical examination, they were reported as being the bones of a powerfully built male, perhaps sixty-five or seventy years old—the legendary age of Peter at his death.

Years later, scientists concluded that the bones Kirschbaum found were a mixture of human and animal remains. This posed no great problem, however, since animals were often on display at Nero's circuses and could have easily mingled with the bones in the cemetery. Also, if Peter's burial had been hurried, placing him in an already occupied tomb would have secured its secrecy. Though controversial, the bones were still believed to belong to Peter. In 1968, Pope Paul IV said, "The relics of St. Peter have been identified in a manner which we believe convincing. . . . Very patient and accurate investigations were made with a result which we believe positive."[6]

What was puzzling, however, was that these bones were not found in Peter's tomb, but rather next to it, wrapped in purple cloth. John Walsh, an authority on the history of Peter's bones, convincingly argues that from the beginning, "Peter's burial was and remained a hidden one."[7] Under the emperor Valerian from 250 to 260, persecutions raged through Rome, and he forbade access to Christian cemeteries. The moving of Peter's bones would have been necessary for their survival. He further argues that the features surrounding Peter's grave beneath the basilica floor could have been an actual church, complete with a baptistry, burial ground, courtyard and altar. "This whole deceptive clutter of brick and tile and marble was nothing less than the first true cathedral," he argues, "an anticipation in miniature of the great guardian structure which still today soars, exuberantly, indestructibly, above its cherished ruins."[8]

I looked through the narrow opening of the repository where the bones were encased in a plastic box, divided into several transparent receptacles. Could it really be true? Could these really be the remains of Simon Peter? I had my doubts, but I also had my hopes. What if? What if these were the remains that walked on water? What if these were the bones that Jesus knew? What if these were the hands that healed the sick and cast out demons. What if?

I savored the moment for as long as I could and wondered what Peter would say to us if he were alive. Perhaps he would remind us that following Christ is a costly business. Perhaps he would address us as he did the Christians in Asia and Galatia: "Dear friends, I urge you, as aliens and strangers in the world" (1 Peter 2:11). But perhaps he would point, like John the Baptist, not to himself but to the Christ who called him to become a fisher of men.

It has been 1,915 years since Peter died, but Peter is not dead. After being crucified upside down, Peter entered heaven right-side up. The hope he had and the faith he knew encourages us all in our struggles. He tells us, "Now for a little while you may have had to suffer grief in all kinds of trials. These have come so that your faith—of greater worth than gold, which perishes even though refined by fire—may be proved genuine and may result in praise, glory and honor when Jesus Christ is revealed" (1 Peter 1:6-7). I looked once more at his dry, bleached bones before being ushered into the crypt of the popes. "See you soon," I said, turning away. "See you soon."

The warm sunshine shocked our systems as we exited the church. Our eyes had grown so accustomed to the darkness of the *scavi* that we squinted all the way back to our hotel. We spent the next few days visiting churches and other sacred sites, but my mind was stuck beneath the basement of Saint Peter's Basilica, gazing at those ancient bones of Peter.

Part of me is still down there even now, listening to their silent testimony. They remind me to take seriously my calling as a Christian. They persuade me that suffering is only for a season, heaven doesn't have hospitals, and one day I will receive a new body that is not susceptible to the difficulties of this life. Above all, they give me hope that the final voyage home will be unlike any other—it will be the last. And waiting for me there will be the God who named me Christian and gave me Christ.

HOMEWARD BOUND

David once told his best friend, Jonathan, "There is only a step between me and death" (1 Samuel 20:3). I often ask myself if I am prepared to take that step. During World War II, preacher and author Helmut Thielicke resisted the ideology of Hitler. Like Bonhoeffer, Thielicke's name was added to the list of those ordered to be executed. One by one, the Nazis captured each person on the list. When they got to the last name, however, it was smudged beyond recognition. Both Bonhoeffer and Thielicke were sentenced to death, but because of a simple smudge, Thielicke's life was spared.

Perhaps we are all a smudge away from death. Would it take more than a car accident or a heart attack? Death is an inevitable outcome for our fallen race. Spurgeon once said, "The young may die; the old must."[9] But death is not the end. It's just a semicolon, a momentary pause in the sentence of life before we are ushered into the presence of the author of the paragraph.

The discipline of pilgrimage prepares us to die. At the end of the adventure, after the arduous task of traveling is over, all that remains is the journey home. One of my favorite pilgrimage experiences was the short flight from Atlanta to Birmingham after having come from a long trip overseas. Maybe it was the peaceful hum of the engine, or perhaps the midnight sky sprinkled with the lights of my city below. Whatever the reason, this was a time of deep reflection. The highs and lows of pilgrimage require a time for contemplation, a time for digesting the lessons and the memories. It is a time to cement in our consciousness what Christ has taught us. For me, going home is one of the best parts of the journey.

Pilgrimage reminds us that one day we will all be going home. The great question mark of death curves around us, and when we think about it, we are afraid. When we talk about death, we talk about mystery. We talk about the unobservable—the not yet but the soon to be. Oh, how we would stop the sand at the top of our hourglass from falling, but grain by grain it goes, minute by minute passes until we are left with just one more pilgrimage in our earthly life.

But death is not the end. When Richard Baxter lay dying on his deathbed, his friends visited him. "Dear Mr. Baxter," they said. "How are you?" "Almost well," he said. "Death cures; it is the best medicine, for they who die are not only almost well, but healed forever."[10]

With great boldness, Christians can look death in the eye and ask, "Where, O death, is your victory? Where, O death, is your sting?" (1 Corinthians 15:55). Death is nothing more than a buzzing bumblebee without a stinger because Christ has conquered death. Jesus Christ empathizes with our sufferings because he himself suffered. He is the alpha and omega, the first and the last, the beginning and the end. He sits in the engine room and the caboose, traveling before us and behind us on this journey called life.

Jonathan Edwards once wrote, "Be content to pass through all difficulties in the way to heaven. . . . What is it in comparison of the sweet rest which is at the end of your journey?"[11] In his poem "Death Be Not Proud," John Donne reminds us that death cannot live forever:

Death be not proud, though some have called thee
Mighty and dreadful, for, thou art not so. . . .
One short sleep past, we wake eternally,
and death shall be no more; death, thou shalt die.[12]

The journey from the womb does not end in the tomb. It cannot, for Jesus promised to prepare a place for his pilgrims, and he is not in the business of betraying. God does not promise rainbows only to give us Skittles. He does not promise mountains only to show us molehills. The promises of God are good and true, and Christians can be confident that death will be with us as it was with Enoch, a saint who walked with God all the way up the highway to heaven.

Some question marks are too curvy to ignore. What is the deepest desire of my heart? Is there a purpose for me on this planet? For what should I be yearning, trusting, loving, seeking, hoping? Questions like these nag and gnaw, throbbing at the center of our souls. It is possible, I suppose, to suppress them by pretending they do not exist. But like a whale in need of air, they will eventually surface. And when we meet them, we must answer them.

Pilgrimage reminds us of our purpose and prepares us for what lies ahead.

In the classic film *The Wizard of Oz,* Judy Garland plays Dorothy, a girl who traveled through a land that was not her home. She was a pilgrim, following the yellow brick road. It was a strange land—a land of tin men, scarecrows and munchkins. There were obstacles to overcome and witches to watch out for, not to mention the lions and tigers and bears (oh my!). But Dorothy knew that as long as she stayed on the path, Kansas would be around the corner. Turns out Oz wasn't all it was cracked up to be, and at the very end of the movie, Dorothy taps her shoes together and says those unforgettable words: "There's no place like home. There's no place like home. There's no place like home."

At the end of our lives we might forget everything we ever learned—the thoughts of great thinkers, the art of great artists, the poems of great poets, the inventions of great inventors, the teachings of great teachers, the music of great musicians, the words of great sentences, the letters of great words, even the alphabet of great letters. We might forget our friends, our neighbors and even the names of our pets. But there is one thing in this world worth remembering: We are going home. And pilgrimage will fuse with paradise, somewhere over the rainbow.

Hear our voice, and grant insight and strength so that we may always respond to hatred with love, to injustice with total dedication to justice, to need with the sharing of self, to war with peace. O God, hear our voice and grant unto the world your everlasting peace.

POPE JOHN PAUL II

EPILOGUE

On the Road Again

We shall not cease from exploration
and the end of all our exploring
will be to arrive where we started
and know the place for the first time.

T. S. ELIOT

Many things are destined to dissolve—a morning mist, an evening breeze, a cup of Häagen-Dazs ice cream sitting on a sunny dashboard. This world is full of them, these things that do not last.

The discipline of pilgrimage prepares us to embrace the eternal within the temporary. It reminds us that life is brief and calls us to live not as tourists, nomads or pedestrians but as pilgrims who walk the stranger's way. The cradle and the coffin are cut from the same tree, and with David we agree, "As for mortals, their days are like grass" (Psalm 103:15 NRSV).

After the long journey, Christian in *Pilgrim's Progress* finally reached the Celestial City. The adventure that began with a burden ended with a blessing, and though his path was filled with potholes, dangers and difficulties, he arrived safely at his home on the horizon.

But Bunyan's story does not end here. Christian's wife, Christiana, followed her husband's example and fled the City of Destruction. With her little children by her side, she embarked on her own pilgrimage toward the heavenly palace. Her travels were hard and her troubles were many, but after crossing the River Jordan, she found her husband waiting with hands out-stretched and arms opened wide. She was finally home.

The practice of pilgrimage promotes community. It builds friendships, creates memories and dissolves barriers between believers. Pilgrimage changes us from the inside out.

A Chinese proverb says, "He who returns from a journey is not the same as he who left."[1] Informed by other cultures, customs and creeds, pilgrimage expands our knowledge of God and increases our appreciation for the spiritual disciplines. Giving flexibility to the often stiff body of Christ, it allows the hands of God to touch the feet of God so we may stretch and run together with perseverance the race marked out for us. To this end, Jesus' prayer for unity—"that they may be one" (John 17:11)—is fulfilled.

The smell of freshly mowed grass filled my little lungs. I was six years old, standing next to my father in the middle of an empty soccer field. It was late in the morning, but the grass was still wet from the midnight dew. It was the green season of my life, when the world looks as bright as it did when God first created it. My father and I walked to the edge of the field where faded lines marked the perimeter of the rectangle. This was a well-worn field. Weeks of running players, screaming coaches and lemonade-bearing soccer moms had blurred its boundaries.

My father handed me a can of white spray paint and showed me how to use it. Hissing paint sprayed erratically from the cold aluminum can, but eventually I learned to spray a smooth line. Around the field I went, spraying a fresh layer of paint on top of the old one. As I turned the last corner, a thought struck me: This line was not my own. I didn't invent the boundaries of this field; its measurements were made by someone long before me; its angles and corners were already calculated. My job was simply to clarify them for future players.

The fading lines of pilgrimage have all but disappeared from the field of Christian history, but perhaps they can be resprayed. Perhaps they can be redefined for modern pilgrims. Like a precious pearl at the bottom of the sea, pilgrimage waits to be discovered by those who are willing to journey to the depths. I promise the destination is worth the dive.

From the perimeter of a soccer field, my father and I traveled around the circumference of the globe. We continue to journey to sacred cities and ancient castles, walking the steps that history warmed beneath our feet. Once in a while, when my backpack sits dormant in my room and my walking shoes grow cold in my closet, I'll pull out my old, trusty atlas and find the map of Jerusalem. Its wrinkled pages are yellowed, its binding is brittle, but I'll open it anyway and dream of going there. For some time I have longed to see that sacred city where my Lord decided to live. I want to walk its streets, breathe its air and pray in the gardens where great drops of sweat became great drops of blood. It is a dream worth dreaming, a thought worth thinking and a pilgrimage worth writing home about. "If dreams are just like wine," Gershwin once said, "then I am drunk with mine."

Perhaps I'll meet you there and we'll walk together on the ancient paths. You'll have to forgive me for stopping at every site in view and looking at every view in sight. But I'm sure our paths will cross.

Until then, God bless, bon voyage, and many blessings on your sacred travels.

APPENDIX

Traveling Tips and Pilgrimage Sites

The following is a select list of resources that can be helpful in planning a pilgrimage. I have included books on potential pilgrimage sites and traveling tips. This list is by no means exhaustive, but perhaps it will be a blessing to you as you practice the ancient discipline of pilgrimage.

Books

The Journey: A Guide for the Modern Pilgrim
Maria Ruiz Scaperlanda and Michael Scaperlanda
Loyola Press, 2004

The Art of Pilgrimage: The Seeker's Guide to Making Travel Sacred
Phil Cousineau
Conari, 1998

The Way of the Lord: Christian Pilgrimage Today
Tom Wright
Eerdmans, 1999

Walking the Bible: A Journey by Land through the Five Books of Moses
Bruce Feiler
HarperCollins, 2005

*On the Road with Francis of Assisi: A Timeless Journey Through Umbria
and Tuscany, and Beyond*
Linda Bird Francke
Random House, 2005

American Pilgrimage: Eleven Sacred Journeys and Spiritual Destinations
Mark Oglibee and Jana Riess
Paraclete, 2006

*The Spiritual Traveler: Boston and New England: A Guide to Sacred Sites
and Peaceful Places*
Jana Riess
HiddenSpring, 2002

Websites
www.taize.fr (The community of Taizé, France)
www.glenstal.org (The community of Glenstal Abbey in Limerick,
   Ireland)
www.iona.org.uk (The community of Iona, Scotland)

ACKNOWLEDGMENTS

I would like to thank all the pilgrims who have gone the extra mile to encourage, support and sustain me through the writing of this book:

My wife, Rebecca, who with great patience and understanding sacrificed for, nurtured and edited this book from conception to maturity. The path is so much sweeter with you beside me.

My father, Timothy George, who instilled within me a deep appreciation for the things of God. My mother, Denise George, who gave me a passion for words and clothes me with prayers, friendship and godly wisdom. My parents-in-law, Jerry and Bayne Pounds, who love and support me with unprecedented graciousness and provided quiet places to write. My sister, Alyce, and brother-in-law, Jerry Jr., who were springboards for my thoughts.

All my allies and advocates at InterVarsity Press, especially Al Hsu, my editor, whose direction and expertise contributed to the writing of this book. And Andy Le Peau, for taking a chance on a young writer.

The great writers, thinkers, preachers and teachers who have shaped my theology, worship and discipleship. J. I. Packer, a beloved mentor and champion of the faith, who taught me the importance of biblical theology. Chuck Colson, who communicates the gospel with zeal and relevance. And James Earl Massey, a great expositor of the Scriptures.

Billy Kim, for heavenly hospitality in South Korea. Fenton Lyons, a monk, scholar and friend who was Jesus to me in Ireland. Earl Potts, who has run the race so very well. Fran Sciacca, a prophet who taught me to live as an alien and a pilgrim in this land. David Riker, who trekked the world with me. Norfleete Day, who gave me an appreciation for spiritual formation. Calvin Miller, who taught me to think creatively. And Robert Smith Jr., who pulls me into the presence of God with his prayers.

The faculty, staff, students and administration of Beeson Divinity School for endless encouragement and enthusiasm.

And, of course, the creators of Crocs, the best traveling shoe ever invented.

Soli Deo Gloria

NOTES

Introduction: To Be a Pilgrim

[1]Richard Foster, *Celebration of Discipline* (SanFrancisco: HarperSanFrancisco, 1998), p. 1.

Chapter One: Pilgrims in the Process

[1]Geoffrey Chaucer, *The Canterbury Tales* (Franklin Center, Penn.: Franklin Library, 1981), p. 3.

[2]Richard Foster, *Celebration of Discipline* (San Francisco: HarperSanFrancisco, 1998), p. 1.

[3]Oswald Chambers, *My Utmost for His Highest* (New York: Dodd, Mead, 1935), p. 202.

Chapter Three: In the Steps of Luther

[1]Quoted in Sarah York, *Pilgrim Heart: The Inner Journey Home* (San Francisco: Jossey-Bass, 2001), p. 1.

[2]Martin Luther, "A Mighty Fortress," in *Baptist Hymnal*, ed. Grady C. Cothen (Nashville: Convention Press, 1975), p. 8.

[3]Esther de Waal, *Seeking God: The Way of St. Benedict* (Collegeville, Minn.: Liturgical Press, 1984), p. 82.

Chapter Four: The Way to Assisi

[1]Henri Nouwen, *Here and Now: Living in the Spirit* (New York: Crossroad, 1994), p. 111.

[2]Ibid., p. 130.

[3]Henri Nouwen, *The Inner Voice of Love: A Journey Through Anguish to Freedom* (New York: Image Books, 1998), p. 59.

[4]"Barna Reviews Top Religious Trends of 2005," The Barna Update, www.barna.org, December 20, 2005.

Chapter Five: In Search of Spurgeon

[1]Charles Spurgeon, *My Conversion* (New Kensington, Penn.: Whitaker House, 1996), p. 38.

[2]Charles Haddon Spurgeon: *Autobiography I: The Early Years* (Avon, U.K.: Banner of Truth Trust, 1994), p. 149.

[3]Tom Wright, *The Way of the Lord: Christian Pilgrimage Today* (Grand Rapids: Eerdmans, 1999), p. 13.

[4]Charles Spurgeon, *The Power of the Cross of Christ* (Lynnwood, Wash.: Emerald Books, 1995), p. 79.

[5]Louis A. Drummond, *Spurgeon: Prince of Preachers* (Grand Rapids: Kregel, 1992), p. 751.

[6]Ibid., p. 753.

Chapter Six: Amazing Grace

[1]Steve Turner, *Amazing Grace: The Story of America's Most Beloved Song* (New York: HarperCollins, 2002), p. 28.

[2]John Newton, *Out of the Depth* (Grand Rapids: Kregel, 1990), p. 71.

[3]Ibid., p. 80.

[4]Henri Nouwen, *The Way of the Heart* (San Francisco: HarperSanFrancisco, 1991), p. 50.

[5]Thomas Merton, *The Wisdom of the Desert: Sayings from the Desert Fathers of the Fourth Century* (New York: New Directions, 1960), p. 30.

[6]Martin Luther King Jr., "Letter from a Birmingham Jail," <http://almaz.com/nobel/peace/MLK-jail.html>, accessed August 16, 2006.

[7]www.quotationspage.com/quotes/Martin_Luther_King_Jr.

[8]Nouwen, *Way of the Heart*, p. 59.

[9]Ibid., p. 30.

[10]Barbara Brown Taylor, *When God Is Silent* (Boston: Cowley, 1998), p. 29.

Chapter Seven: From Sunshine to Shadow

[1]Elisabeth Raum, *Dietrich Bonhoeffer: Called by God* (New York: Continuum, 2002), p. 65.

²Ibid., p. 150.

³Dietrich Bonhoeffer, *The Cost of Discipleship*, trans. R. H. Fuller (New York: Macmillan, 1949), p. 38.

⁴Ibid., p. 47.

⁵Raum, *Dietrich Bonhoeffer*, p. 151.

⁶Ibid., p. 149.

⁷Bonhoeffer, *Cost of Discipleship*, p. 99.

⁸Barbara Brown Taylor, *When God Is Silent* (Boston: Cowley, 1998), p. 72.

⁹Bonhoeffer, *Cost of Discipleship*, p. 16.

¹⁰Ibid., p. 20.

¹¹If you have been diagnosed with this or any other digestive disease (Crohn's, IBD, etc.), I recommend Jordan Rubin's *Patient Heal Thyself* (Topanga, Calif.: Freedom, 2003). It offers tremendous encouragement and help.

¹²"His Eye is on the Sparrow," *African American Heritage Hymnal* (Chicago: GIA, 2001), p. 143.

¹³Timothy George, *John Calvin and the Church: A Prism of Reform* (Louisville, Ky.: Westminster John Knox Press, 1990), p. 68.

¹⁴Eugene G. Peterson, *A Long Obedience in the Same Direction: Discipleship in an Instant Society* (Downers Grove, Ill.: InterVarsity Press, 1980), p. 34.

¹⁵A. W. Tozer, *Gems from Tozer: Selections from the Writings of A. W. Tozer* (Camp Hill, Penn.: Christian Publications, 1969), p. 42.

¹⁶Misty Bernall, *She Said Yes: The Unlikely Martyrdom of Cassie Bernall* (Nashville: Word, 1999), p. 13.

Chapter Eight: Thin Places

¹Adomnán of Iona, *Life of St Columba* (London: Penguin Books, 1995), p. 176.

²Bernard Meehan, *The Book of Kells: An Illustrated Introduction to the Manuscript in Trinity College Dublin* (London: Thames & Hudson, 2002), p. 29.

³Robert E. Webber, *The Younger Evangelicals* (Grand Rapids: Baker, 2002), p. 92.

Chapter Nine: Saints, Swords and Samurai

¹D.C. Talk, *Jesus Freaks: Stories of Revolutionaries Who Changed their World* (Minneapolis: Bethany House, 2002), p. 41.

²Thomas Clearly, *Code of the Samurai: A Modern Translation of the Bushido Shoshinshu*

of Taira Shigesuke (Tokyo: Tuttle, 1999), p. 60.

[3]Francois Fénelon, *Talking With God* (Brewster, Mass.: Paraclete, 1997), p. 5.

[4]Oswald Chambers, *If You Will Ask: Reflections on the Power of Prayer* (Grand Rapids: Discovery House, 1958), p. 20.

[5]Henri Nouwen, *The Way of the Heart* (San Francisco: HarperSanFrancisco, 1991), p. 59.

[6]Dudley Hall, *Incense and Thunder* (Sisters, Ore.: Multnomah, 1999), p. 27.

[7]C. S. Lewis. *Grief* (Nashville: Thomas Nelson, 1998), p. 34.

[8]Morihei Ueshiba, *The Art of Peace* (London: Shambhala, 2002), p. 18.

[9]Bruce Lee, *The Tao of Gung Fu: A Study in the Way of Chinese Martial Art* (Tokyo: Tuttle, 1997), pp. 129, 138.

Chapter Ten: Sacred Songs

[1]"That little springtime! John Paul II in Taizé," <www.taize.fr/en_article63.html>.

[2]Ibid.

[3]*Songs and Prayers from Taizé* (Chicago: GIA, 1991).

[4]"A Soul Attentive to Preparing a Future of Peace," <www.taize.fr/en_article 1776.html>.

[5]"That little springtime! John Paul II in Taizé," <www.taize.fr/en_article63.html>.

[6]Pliny the Younger, quoted in J. McKinnon, *Music in Early Christian Literature* (Cambridge: Cambridge University Press, 1986), p. 27.

[7]Saint Augustine, quoted in McKinnon, *Music*, p. 158.

[8]Martin Luther, quoted in F. Blume, *Protestant Church Music* (London: W. W. Norton, 1974), p. 10.

[9]*A Directory for the Publique Worship of God,* in *Reliquiæ Liturgicæ*, vol. 3, *The Parliamentary Directory* (Bath: Binns and Goodwin, 1847).

[10]Charles Spurgeon, *2200 Quotations from the Writings of Charles H. Spurgeon,* ed. Tom Carter (Grand Rapids: Baker, 1988), p. 130.

[11]Ecroyd Claxton, quoted in D. J. Epstein, *Sinful Tunes and Spirituals: Black Folk Music to the Civil War* (Urbana: University of Illinois Press, 1977), p. 9.

[12]"I Want Jesus to Walk with Me," in *African American Heritage Hymnal* (Chicago: GIA, 2001), p. 563.

Chapter Eleven: Breaking Bread with the Benedictines

[1]Kathleen Norris, *The Cloister Walk* (New York: Riverhead, 1996), p. 7.

[2]*The Rule of Saint Benedict*, trans. Anthony C. Meisel and M. L. Mastro (Garden City, N.Y.: Image, 1975), p. 89.

[3]Alexander Schmemann, *For the Life of the World: Sacraments and Orthodoxy* (Crestwood, N.Y.: St. Vladimir's Seminary Press, 1973), p. 16.

[4]Esther de Waal, *Seeking God: The Way of St. Benedict* (Collegeville, Minn.: Liturgical, 1984), p. 121.

[5]Henri Nouwen, *The Return of the Prodigal Son: The Story of Homecoming* (New York: Doubleday, 1994), p. 106.

Chapter Twelve: A Glimpse of Glory

[1]Elisabeth Elliot, *The Journals of Jim Elliot* (Old Tappan, N.J.: Fleming H. Revell, 1978), p. 72.

[2]Elisabeth Elliot, *Through Gates of Splendor* (Old Tappan, N.J.: Fleming H. Revell, 1970), p. 200.

[3]Elliot, *Journals*, p. 222.

[4]*Amsterdam 2000: Proclaiming Peace and Hope for the New Millennium* (Minneapolis: Billy Graham Evangelistic Association, 2001), p. 28.

[5]Ibid., p. 31.

[6]Ibid., p. 31.

[7]J. I. Packer, *A Quest for Godliness* (Wheaton, Ill.: Crossway, 1990), p. 215.

[8]Elliot, *Journals*, p. 309.

Chapter Thirteen: Roaming Through Rome

[1]Tacitus, quoted in John Evangelist Walsh, *The Bones of St. Peter: The First Full Account of the Search for the Apostle's Body* (Garden City, N.Y.: Doubleday, 1982), p. 36.

[2]Walsh, *Bones of St. Peter*, p. 20.

[3]"Acts 12:12-19" in *The Broadman Bible Commentary*, ed. Clifton J. Allen (Nashville: Broadman, 1970), 10:77.

[4]Walsh, *Bones of St. Peter*, p. 21.

[5]Ibid., p. 37.

[6]Ibid., p. 2.

[7]Ibid., p. 132.

[8]Ibid., p. 146.

[9]Charles Spurgeon, *2200 Quotations from the Writings of Charles H. Spurgeon*, ed.

Tom Carter (Grand Rapids: Baker, 1988), p. 49.

[10]Quoted in *2200 Quotations*, p. 51.

[11]Quoted in Stephen J. Nichols, *Jonathan Edwards: A Guided Tour of His Life and Thought* (Phillipsburg, N.J.: P & R, 2001), p. 230.

[12]John T. Shawcross, ed., *The Complete Poetry of John Donne* (Garden City, N.Y.: Doubleday, 1967), p. 342.

Epilogue: On the Road Again

[1]Maria Ruiz Scaperlanda and Michael Scaperlanda, *The Journey: A Guide for the Modern Pilgrim* (Chicago: Loyola Press, 2004), p. 202.